Worldwide Interesting

WORLDWIDE INTERESTING PEOPLE

162 History Makers of African Descent

George L. Lee

with a foreword by
DR. HELEN E. WILLIAMS

McFarland & Company, Inc., Publishers
Jefferson, North Carolina, and London

To my late wife, Jennie; my son, Richard;
my granddaughter, Terri; my late brother, Bill;
my great-granddaughter, Corryn;
and my great-granddaughter, Camille

*The present work is a reprint of the library bound edition
of* Worldwide Interesting People: 162 History Makers of
African Descent, *first published in 1992 by McFarland.*

LIBRARY OF CONGRESS CATALOGUING-IN-PUBLICATION DATA

Lee, George L., 1906–
    Worldwide interesting people : 162 history makers of African
descent / George L. Lee ; foreword by Helen E. Williams.
        p.   cm.
    Includes bibliographical references and index.

    ISBN 978-0-7864-6768-6
    softcover : acid free paper ∞

    1. Blacks—Biography—Juvenile literature.   2. Africans—
Biography—Juvenile literature.   3. Afro-Americans—Biography—
Juvenile literature.   4. Leadership—Juvenile literature.
[1. Blacks—Biography.   2. Afro-Americans—Biography.
3. Africa—Biography.]   I. Title.
CT107.L46 2012   [B]   920'.009296—920   91-50939

BRITISH LIBRARY CATALOGUING DATA ARE AVAILABLE

Front cover: *clockwise from top left* Philippa Schuyler, Tim Moore,
Florence Mills, Capt. Adrian Richardson; *center* Joel A. Rogers.
Back cover: *top* Mary Eugenia Charles; *bottom* Sir Ladapo
Ademola

Manufactured in the United States of America

McFarland & Company, Inc., Publishers
    Box 611, Je›erson, North Carolina 28640
    www.mcfarlandpub.com

Foreword

"Advocacy" means supporting, encouraging, inspiring, or promoting in any of a variety of ways. Usually, the advocate uses a strategy which feels comfortable and empowering, because the effort required to advocate is typically prolonged and demands dedicated attention to a specific goal. Literature is often a medium through which advocates state their case to broadly dispersed audiences. It is appropriate that this is so because literature mirrors individuals and their efforts in responding to and creating traditions for future generations.

Such is the case of this book; it is advocative in its essence. Its conception began decades ago when author and illustrator George Lee saw a need for collected information about black achievers worldwide. In addressing this need, he became an advocate for the dissemination of information regarding peoples whose traditions of achievement had been largely unheralded. The author seems to understand that a look into our past can help us in designing the present for future benefits. He, too, encountered and overcame difficulties and discouragements familiar to all minority group advocates who promote minority group interests and achievements. This book demonstrates how well he overcame obstacles with artistic talent and persistent research. The result is a valuable statement for readers of all ages and cultural backgrounds.

Each reader is encouraged to understand the value of this book to young people who are still impressionable and in need of text and illustrations with which to enhance their thoughts about themselves and their culture, and to improve the quality of their activities and lives. Encouraging youths to think about why people do what they do and encouraging the search for effects as well as causes often lead to avid reading spurts for personal gratification.

The advocacy of reading is a wonderfully valuable component of any effort to foster cultural understanding. The enhancement of pride in origins, contributions, and culture (however widely spread) is a reward which all

Foreword

parents, writers, educators, and readers should aspire to obtain and more fully appreciate. This book contributes greatly to any personal goals which its intended audience might choose to pursue.

May everyone enjoy the learning adventure this book represents.

Dr. Helen E. Williams
Fall 1991

Contents

Table of Contents

Table of Contents

Introduction

My career as a newspaper artist began soon after I arrived in Chicago in 1927. With no formal art education my thinking was school—perhaps a commercial art school. I applied at the Vogue Art School and was politely told that they did not accept Negro students. So I enrolled at the Art Institute, but withdrew when I found I didn't like figure drawing. I had been fascinated by sports drawings in newspapers so I turned to the papers and sports. Much of my initial work involved the sports world and is documented in the book *Interesting Athletes* (McFarland, 1990).

The drawings in the present work are from my black press feature, "Interesting People," which I created in 1945 and suspended in 1948 due to the shortage of newsprint right after World War II. In 1970 I resumed "Interesting People" after retirement from a 33-year career with the U.S. Postal Service. The purpose of the feature was to highlight the achievements of African Americans. I kept files on all the information I came across in the media about anyone that I thought was interesting. Therefore the facts here are not the type of information you will find in other books. I continued drawing the feature until 1986 when I retired at the age of 80.

This collection along with *Interesting People* (1989), *Interesting Athletes* (1990), and *Inspiring African Americans* (1991)—all published by McFarland & Company, Inc.—form a virtually complete record of "Interesting People," my syndicated feature. "Interesting People" and therefore the pages of this book have appeared in leading black newspapers throughout the United States, such as the *Afro-American* (Baltimore), and the *Miami Times*.

Worldwide Interesting People is arranged in approximate chronological order according to the life dates of the persons depicted. My other books have focused on those African Americans who have made their achievements in the United States. The emphasis in this book is on those who may have been born outside the United States or those who gained international fame or those whose life and achievements have little to do with

Worldwide Interesting People

the United States (such as Iris King, the first woman mayor of Kingston, Jamaica). This book also differs from my others in that it includes a few drawings that feature important people from the distant past, such as Piankhi, an Ethiopian ruler of ancient Egypt.

This book is intended to provide interesting stories about people of achievement. May each reader find a source of inspiration within these pages.

George L. Lee

ACCORDING to HISTORIANS

PIANKHI

THE GREATEST OF THE 18 ETHIOPIAN RULERS OF ANCIENT EGYPT. LEAVING HIS COUNTRY IN 750 B.C. HIS WARRIORS CONQUERED ALL EGYPT TO THE MOUTH OF THE NILE. PIANKHI WAS THE FIRST TO USE CALVARY IN WARFARE. GIVING HIM SUPERIORITY. THE POWERFUL ETHIOPIANS OF SUDAN HAVE A REMARKABLE HISTORY. PIANKHI, KING OF NUBIA DURING THE FIRST MILENNIUM BEFORE THE ADVENT OF CHRISTIANITY, PLOTTED AND PLANNED TO CONQUER EGYPT FOR MANY YEARS BEFORE HIS MIGHTY ARMIES MADE THE MASSIVE INVASION AND TAKE-OVER. HE WAS DETERMINED TO END THE EGYPTIAN ... OPPRESSION. EGYPTIAN PHARAOHS FORCED SURROUNDING NATIONS TO PAY TRIBUTES IN THE FORM OF GOLD AND FIGHTING MEN FOR EGYPT'S ARMIES AND SLAVES FOR EGYPT'S OWN NATION-BUILDING. PIANKHI HAD BUILT A WELL-DISCIPLINED ARMY AND STUDIED THE DEFENSES OF ALL TOWNS AND SEAPORTS. UNDER THE GUISE OF BRINGING TRIBUTE TO THE KING OSORKON OF EGYPT, PIANKHI'S TRIUMPHAL MARCH INTO MEMPHIS THE CAPITAL LEFT EGYPT UNDER THE COMPLETE MASTERY AND CONTROL OF THE BLACK KING OF ETHIOPIA.

1982 GEO L. LEE FEATURE SERVICE

3

ACCORDING TO HISTORIANS,

AKHENATON (BERLIN MUSEUM)

AMENHOTEP IV
FIRST WORLD HERO!

BETTER KNOWN AS "AKHENATON THE HERETIC KING" WAS THE MOST EXTRAORDINARY MONARCH OF EGYPT. HIS FEATURES WERE OF NEGROID STRAIN. HIS GENIUS AND HIS FAR REACHING VICTORIES MADE HIM LORD SUPREME OF THE THEN CIVILIZED WORLD. HE PREACHED THE GOSPEL OF PEACE, LOVE, TRUTH AND BROTHERHOOD 1300 YEARS BEFORE CHRIST. HE TAUGHT THE DOCTRINE OF ONE GOD, 2000 YEARS BEFORE MOHAMET. 3,000 YEARS BEFORE DARWIN HE SENSED THE UNITY THAT RUNS THROUGHOUT ALL THE UNIVERSE. HE WAS THE WEALTHIEST MAN ON EARTH. HIS REIGN BEGAN IN 1375 B.C. HE DIED IN HIS 17th YEAR OF HIS REIGN.

THE GREAT PYRAMID OF CHEOPS

CHEOPS, A BLACK KING OF HERODOTUS, BUILT THE GREAT PYRAMID - ONE OF THE 7-WONDERS OF THE ANCIENT WORLD. IT IS 451 FT-HIGH - 2,500,000 BLOCKS OF GRANITE - TOOK 100,000 MEN 30 YEARS TO BUILD. COMPLETED IN 3730 B.C.

Geo. Lee

ACCORDING TO HISTORIANS..

SUNNI ALI
(REIGNED FROM -1464-1492)

WHO ROSE FROM A COMMON SOLDIER TO BECOME A KING OF THE SONGHOI EMPIRE WHICH STRETCHED FROM THE ATLANTIC TO LAKE CHAD IN CENTRAL AFRICA. HIS MILITARY GENIUS CARVED OUT THIS EMPIRE. ONE OF THE GREATEST COMMANDERS OF HIS TIME. IN 1469 HE CAPTURED TIMBUKTU FROM THE TUAREG PEOPLE AND MADE IT THE CAPITAL OF HIS EMPIRE. TIMBUKTU BECAME THE RICHEST MARKET IN WEST AFRICA AND THE CULTURAL CENTER OF THE ISLAMIC WORLD.

Geo Lee

THE MARINIDES, OF THE BENI

MARĪN PERIOD (1213-1471) A BLACK DYNASTY OF MOROCCAN RULERS WERE THE FIRST TO USE GUNPOWDER IN THE WESTERN PART OF THE OLD WORLD. THIS WAS AT THE SIEGE OF TAFILET IN AFRICA IN 1274, 72-YEARS BEFORE ITS USE IN EUROPE BY THE ENGLISH AT THE BATTLE OF CRECY AGAINST THE FRENCH IN 1346 A.D.

ACCORDING to HISTORIANS

JUAN LATINO

KNOWN AS "THE MASTER", WAS ONE OF THE GREATEST OF ALL LATIN SCHOLARS AND ONE OF SPAIN'S LEADING POETS. A BLACK AFRICAN SLAVE BORN IN GUINEA IN 1516. AT 12 HE AND HIS MOTHER WERE TAKEN TO BAEN, SPAIN TO WORK IN THE HOUSE OF DUKE DE SESA. THE BOY SEEMED BRIGHT. THE DUKE HAD HIM EDUCATED. JUAN EXCELLED IN LATIN AND GREEK. HE WAS SENT TO THE UNIV. OF GRANADA WITH SUCH RARE TALENTS HE BECAME THE TUTOR OF YOUNG NOBILITY. IN 1565 APPOINTED THE PROFESSOR OF POETRY AT THE UNIVERSITY. MARRIED ONE OF HIS PUPILS, LADY ANA DE CARJAVAL AND HAD FOUR GIRLS. AFTER HIS FRIEND DON JUAN OF AUSTRIA WON A MILITARY VICTORY OVER THE TURKS IN THE BATTLE OF LEPANTO IN 1571 HE WROTE A REMARKABLE BOOK. IT WAS HIS MOST FAMOUS WORK "THE AUSTRIAD" A POEM OF DON JUAN'S VICTORY. PUBLISHED IN GRANADA (1573) AND WON HIM RESPECT...A SCHOLAR, AND ONE OF THE RAREST LITERARY PRIZES IN THE WORLD! LATINO DIED IN 1599.

1981 GEO L. LEE FEATURE SERVICE

ACCORDING TO HISTORIANS...

BLESSED MARTIN De PORRES

THE FIFTH NEGRO SAINT OF THE CATHOLIC CHURCH. OTHERS WERE—POPE VICTOR I, 189-199; POPE MELCHIADES, 311-314; POPE GELASIUS 492-496; ST. BENEDICT THE MOOR, 1526-1589.

BLESSED MARTIN WAS THE ILLEGITIMATE SON OF DON JUAN De PORRES A SPANISH NOBLEMAN AND ANA MELAS-QUEZ, A NEGRO EX-SLAVE, BORN IN LIMA, PERU ON DEC 9, 1579. ABANDON-ED BY HIS FATHER HE BECAME A SERVANT IN THE CONVENT OF SANTA DOMINGO WHERE HUMBLY HE DID LOWLY TASKS. HE LEARNED TO BEG AND PROVIDED FOR THE SICK AND POOR. AT AGE 24 HE WAS ALLOWED TO BECOME A MONK. HIS CHARITABLE DEEDS AND HIS HEALING MIRACLES MADE HIM FAMOUS. HE DIED AT 60—A SYMBOL OF BROTHERHOOD – THE HIGHEST ACHIEVEMENT OF MAN. HE WAS CANONIZED BY POPE JOHN XXIII IN ST. PETER'S BASILICA, ROME IN MAY, 1962... 323 YEARS AFTER HIS DEATH! "THE SAINT OF THE BROOM."

Geo Lee

S 1975 George L. Lee Feature Service

ACCORDING to HISTORIANS

MOULAY ISMAIL

1647, 1729

THE MIGHTY EMPEROR OF MOROCCO CALLED BY SOME HISTORIANS "THE AFRICAN LOUIS XIV"

THE MOST NOTED RULER OF MOROCCO SINCE THE DAYS OF YAKUB (1286). J.A.ROGERS, HISTORIAN, ONCE WROTE; HIS MOTHER WAS A NEGRO SLAVE. HE HAD 25,000 WHITE SLAVES, CAPTURED ON THE SEAS OR ON THE COASTS OF EUROPE AND THE BRITISH ISLES TO BUILD HIS PALACE AT MEKNES. WITH HIS BLACK GUARDS OR EL BOKHARI, NUMBERING 150,000 HE CONQUERED ALL HIS NEIGHBORS. THE MOST COLOSSAL STABLES OF ALL TIME WERE AT HIS COMMAND. HE HAD 12,000 PURE BLOODED ARAB HORSES. ISMAIL REIGNED 55-YEARS (1672-1727).

THE EMANCIPATOR

BUDDO

BUDDO, ALSO CALLED GENERAL BORDEAUX A FULL-BLOOD NEGRO LED A SUCCESSFUL REVOLT OF SLAVES AGAINST THE PEOPLE OF ST. CROIX, DANISH, W. INDIES (NOW-VIRGIN ISLANDS) AND FORCED THE GOVERNOR-GENERAL TO DECREE AN EMANCIPATION OF ALL SLAVES ON JULY 3, 1848 INCLUDING THE ENTIRE ISLANDS.

GEO LEE

1979 GEO L. LEE FEATURE SERVICE

8

ACCORDING to HISTORIANS

1697
1781

ABRAHAM HANNIBAL

ONE OF THE MOST EXTRAORDINARY BLACK PERSONALITIES OF HIS TIME. TAKEN AS A HOSTAGE FROM HIS PARENTS, THE FATHER A CHIEFTAIN IN NORTHERN ABYSSINIA, AT THE AGE OF 8. SOLD AS A SLAVE IN CONSTANTINOPLE AND BOUGHT AS A GIFT TO PETER THE GREAT OF RUSSIA, WHO ADOPTED THE HIGHLY INTELLIGENT BOY AS HIS GODSON. HE WAS SENT TO PARIS TO STUDY MATHEMATICS AND ENGINEERING. A BRILLIANT ARMY CAREER HE ROSE TO GENERAL-IN-CHIEF OF THE... RUSSIAN ARMY. HE ATTAINED HIGH GOVERNMENT STATUS AND WEALTH!

GEO LEE

IVAN HANNIBAL

ONE OF 5-SONS OF ABRAHAM. DISTINGUISHED FOR HIS VALOR AND STRATEGIC SKILL. ADMIRAL OF A MILITARY FLEET, HE DEFEATED THE TURKS AT THE BATTLE OF NAVARIN IN 1770. GOVERNOR OF THE UKRAINE, RUSSIA. FOUNDED THE CITY AND BUILDER OF THE FORTRESS OF KHERSON. ROSE TO MAJOR GENERAL. DIED 1801.

1979 GEO L. LEE FEATURE SERVICE

ACCORDING to HISTORIANS

SAM FRAUNCES,

BETTER KNOWN AS "BLACK SAM" WAS BORN IN THE WEST INDIES. HE WENT TO NEW YORK CITY AND BECAME A TAVERN-KEEPER. GEORGE WASHINGTON AND REVOLUTIONARY LEADERS DINED DAILY AT "BLACK SAM'S" INN THE "QUEEN'S HEAD." THEY DISCUSSED PLANS FOR THE LIBERATION OF AMERICA. FRAUNCES WHO CONTRIBUTED LARGE SUMS TO THE CAUSE WAS PUBLICLY THANKED BY THE CONGRESS. LATER HE SERVED AS HEAD OF THE HOUSEHOLD FOR PRES. WASHINGTON. FRAUNCES'S FAMED TAVERN IS NOW A HISTORIC MUSEUM (NYC). DIED OCT 1795.

THE DUKE OF FLORENCE
ALESSANDRO DE' MEDICI

HIS MOTHER, ANNA A NEGRO SERVANT GIRL OF CALAVECCHIO, ITALY, WIFE OF A WHITE MULE DRIVER, BECAME THE CONCUBINE OF POPE CLEMENT VII. THUS THE BIRTH OF ALESSANDRO IN 1511. HE BECAME THE REIGNING DUKE OF FLORENCE, MARRIED MARGARET ONLY DAUGHTER OF EMPEROR CHARLES V IN 1536.

1978 GEO L. LEE FEATURE SERVICE

ACCORDING TO HISTORIANS

JEAN BAPTISTE POINT DUSABLE

A NATIVE OF SANTO DOMINGO WAS BORN ABOUT 1750. HE LEFT HAITI AND CAME TO THE NEW WORLD AND SETTLED IN LOUISIANA NEAR THE MISSISSIPPI RIVER. A FREE NEGRO HE CAME UP THE RIVER TO ILLINOIS AND LIVED AMONG THE PEORIA INDIANS BEFORE SETTLING ON THE CHICAGO RIVER WHERE IT JOINED LAKE MICHIGAN. HE SET UP A TRADING POST

AND MADE A FORTUNE BY TRADING WITH THE INDIANS FOR FURS. HE CALLED IT... CHICAGO FROM THE INDIAN WORD - ESCHICAGOU. HE MARRIED AN INDIAN GIRL AND THEY HAD TWO CHILDREN. DUSABLE BUILT THE FIRST CABIN WHICH LED TO A GREAT CITY - CHICAGO, THE NATION'S SECOND LARGEST. FOUNDED BY A BLACK MAN IN 1779. HE DIED IN 1818 AND WAS BURIED IN ST. CHARLES, MO.

11

ACCORDING TO HISTORIANS

1745·1799

MONS. CHEVALIER DE ST. GEORGES

ONE OF FRANCE'S MOST NOTED BLACKS. BORN IN GUADE-LOUPE, W.I., ON CHRISTMAS DAY, THE SON OF A SLAVE MOTHER AND THE MARQUIS DE LANGLEY. HE FLED TO FRANCE AND BECAME THE IDOL OF NOBILITY. A FASCINATING FIGURE IN THE COURTS OF EUR-OPE. AN ACCOMPLISHED VIOLINIST, PIANIST AND COMPOSER OF NOTE, A POET, ACTOR AND DRA-MATIST. A SKILLFUL SWORDSMAN THE BEST OF HIS TIME; AS A MARKSMAN HE COULD FIRE OFF PISTOLS WITH BOTH HANDS AND HIT BOTH PIGEONS; AS A SOLDIER AND A COMMANDER HE PERFORMED WELL ON THE FIELD OF BATTLE ; AS A DANCER, HORSEMAN AND SKATER HE WAS GRACEFUL IN A LAND SUPREME FOR ITS ELEGANCE ; IN HIS DRESS HE WAS THE MODEL OF HIS TIME AND SET FASHIONS IN FRANCE AND ENGLAND. HE POSSESSED A SPIRIT OF RAREST GENEROSITY, KINDLINESS AND INTEGRITY. HE WAS IDOLIZED BY HIS COUNTRYMEN..." THE PERFECT GENTLEMAN"... HE DIED IN PARIS AT THE AGE OF 54.

Geo LEE

SLAVE TO POET

1753. 1784

PHILLIS WHEATLEY

A MOST AMAZING PERSON IN THE FIELD OF POETRY. BORN IN SENEGAL, AFRICA AND KIDNAPPED TO AMERICA ON A SLAVE SHIP LANDING AT BOSTON. ONLY ABOUT 8 SHE WAS SOLD TO JOHN WHEATLEY A RELIGIOUS MAN AS A MAID TO HIS WIFE. GIVEN THE NAME OF PHILLIS, THEY BEGAN TO TEACH HER AND WITHIN 16 MONTHS SHE LEARNED TO READ AND WRITE AND SPEAK FLUENT ENGLISH. HER THIRST FOR KNOWLEDGE WAS LIKE ONE "POSSESSED". SHE READ HOMER AND AESCHYLUS TO SHAKESPEARE, MILTON AND THE BIBLE. PHILLIS WROTE HER FIRST POEM AT 14. HER FIRST PUBLISHED WORK IN 1770. A BRILLIANT FUTURE BUT IN POOR HEALTH SHE WAS TAKEN

Geo LEE

IN HIS LETTER OF FEB 28 '76: I THANK YOU SINCERELY FOR YOUR POLITE NOTICE OF ME IN THE ELEGANT LINES YOU ENCLOSED. THE STYLE AND MANNER EXHIBIT A STRIKING PROOF OF YOUR GREAT POETIC TALENTS-THEY MET IN CAMBRIDGE, MASS 1776.

PHILLIS SENT A POEM TO WASHINGTON PRAISING HIM AS COMMANDER-IN-CHIEF OF THE REVOLUTIONARY ARMIES. (1775)

TO LONDON. WHILE THERE HER FIRST BOOK..."POEMS ON VARIOUS SUBJECTS, RELIGIOUS AND MORAL" WAS PUBLISHED BY FRIENDS IN 1773...THE FIRST BLACK AMERICAN WOMAN AND THE SECOND AMERICAN WOMAN. HER POEMS WON HIGH PRAISE FROM SUCH MEN AS.... VOLTAIRE, JOHN HANCOCK, BENJAMIN FRANKLIN AND GEORGE WASHINGTON.

SHAKESPEAREAN

1807
1867

IRA ALDRIDGE

Considered to be the greatest Shakespeapean actor of his day in the European theatre. Born in New York City, the son of an Afro-American mother and an African father. In 1820 he entered the African Free School where he excelled in speech and acting. In 1824 Ira left NYC for England. But being Black kept him in undesirable parts... until 1833, when he received his big break-the title role in "Othello" at the Theatre Royale, Covent Gardens, London. He arose to the heights of greatness. Aldridge toured the Continent and Russia and won the highest honors from kings and rulers. He made-up as a "White-Face" and played... King Lear, Macbeth and the Merchant of Venice. He died on tour in Lodz, Poland at 60.

Geo Lee

© 1987, George L. Lee Feature Service

14

WILLIAM LEIDESDORFF
1810 - 1848

ACCORDING TO HISTORIANS WAS THE FIRST NEGRO MILLIONAIRE IN AMERICA. BORN IN ST. CROIX IN THE DANISH VIRGIN ISLANDS, THE SON OF A DANISH PLANTER AND A NEGRO MOTHER, ANNA MARIE SPARKS. HE WENT TO NEW ORLEANS THEN TO CALIFORNIA. AT THAT TIME MONTEREY WAS THE CAPITAL OF CALIFORNIA WHICH WAS UNDER MEXICAN CONTROL. IN 1844 HE BECAME A MEXICAN CITIZEN. HE ACQUIRED CONSIDERABLE LAND AND WEALTH. THE U.S. TOOK OVER CALIFORNIA IN 1846. MR. LEIDESDORFF ERECTED THE CITY HOTEL IN SAN FRANCISCO WHERE THE FIRST U.S. ELECTIONS WERE HELD. HE WAS NAMED TREASURER. HE OWNED THE FIRST STEAMSHIP TO ENTER THE FRISCO BAY, THE "SITKA" IN NOV. 1847.

Geo Lee

RUDOLPH DUNBAR

THE BRILLIANT COMPOSER- CONDUCTOR WAS THE FIRST BLACK TO LEAD THE FAMOUS BERLIN PHILHARMONIC ORCHESTRA IN ITS 65-YEAR OLD HISTORY, AT THE TITANIA PALAST AUDITORIUM IN BERLIN ON SEPT 2,1945. MR. DUNBAR WAS FOREIGN CORRESPONDENT FOR THE ASSOCIATED NEGRO PRESS DURING WORLD WAR II.

AFRICAN PRINCE

JOSEPH CINQUE
1811 – 1852

HERO OF ONE OF THE MOST DARING EPICS OF THE SEA. CAPTURED IN AFRICA WITH MANY OTHERS AND SOLD INTO SLAVERY IN HAVANA, CUBA IN 1839. THEY WERE PUT ABOARD THE SLAVE SHIP – "AMISTAD" – BOUND FOR THE ISLAND OF PRINCIPE. HE LED A SUCCESSFUL REVOLT AGAINST THE SPANISH CREW. CINQUE ORDERED THE CAPTAIN TO TAKE HIM BACK TO AFRICA BUT WAS TRICKED AND THE SHIP HEADED FOR THE U.S. AND WAS SEIZED BY THE U.S. NAVY. THE SPANISH MINISTER DEMANDED THE SHIP AND SLAVES RETURNED BUT THE U.S. COURTS REFUSED. THE ANTI-SLAVERY PARTY CAME TO THE AID OF THE SLAVES. CINQUE AND HIS GALLANT COMPANIONS WERE TRIED IN THE COURTS OF HARTFORD, CONN. THE "AMISTAD CASE" WENT ALL THE WAY TO THE U.S. SUPREME COURT AND THE SLAVES WERE DEFENDED BY JOHN QUINCY ADAMS. ON MAR 9, 1841 A DECISION GRANTED - FREEDOM!

GEO LEE

© 1972 George L. Lee Feature Service

ALEXANDER CRUMMELL

FAMED EPISCOPALIAN PRIEST, AUTHOR AND EDUCATOR WAS BORN MAR 3, 1819 IN NEW YORK. HE ATTENDED THE FREE AFRICAN SCHOOLS WITH SUCH CLASSMATES AS HENRY GARNET AND IRA ALDRIDGE. ENTERED ONEIDA INSTITUTE AT WHITESBORO, N.Y. A GRADUATE OF CAMBRIDGE UNIV., ENGLAND. SPENT A QUARTER OF A CENTURY IN LIBERIA AND A QUARTER OF A CENTURY IN AMERICA. FOUNDER OF THE AMERICAN NEGRO ACADEMY. ONE OF THE MOST DISTINGUISHED BLACK MEN OF ENGLISH LETTERS IN HIS DAY AND GENERATION AMONG WHITES AND BLACKS.

Geo LEE

ONE OF THE MIGHTIEST OF THE ANTI-SLAVERY ORATORS.

SAMUEL RINGGOLD WARD

BORN IN 1817, IN EASTERN SHORES, MD. SON OF FUGITIVE SLAVE PARENTS WHO WENT TO NEW YORK WHEN HE WAS SMALL AND EDUCATED THERE. HE BECAME A PRESBYTERIAN MINISTER AND PASTORED A WHITE CHURCH. AN ELOQUENT SPEAKER HE WAS EMPLOYED BY THE AMERICAN ANTI-SLAVERY SOCIETY AS A LECTURER IN 1839. HIS BOOK "AUTOBIOGRAPHY OF A FUGITIVE NEGRO".... STIRRED GREAT SYMPATHY FOR THE SLAVES.

GOV. P.B.S. PINCHBACK
1837 - 1921

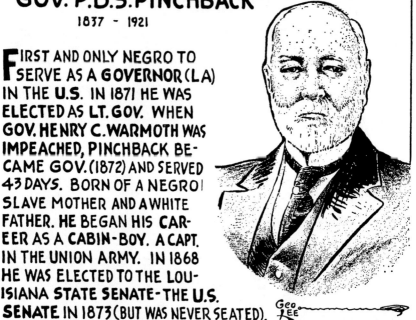

FIRST AND ONLY NEGRO TO SERVE AS A **GOVERNOR** (LA) IN THE **U.S.** IN 1871 HE WAS ELECTED AS **LT. GOV.** WHEN GOV. HENRY C. WARMOTH WAS IMPEACHED, PINCHBACK BE-CAME GOV. (1872) AND SERVED 43 DAYS. BORN OF A NEGRO SLAVE MOTHER AND A WHITE FATHER. HE BEGAN HIS CAR-EER AS A **CABIN-BOY**. A CAPT. IN THE UNION ARMY. IN 1868 HE WAS ELECTED TO THE LOU-ISIANA **STATE SENATE** - THE **U.S. SENATE** IN 1873 (BUT WAS NEVER SEATED).

Geo. LEE

HATTIE M^cDANIEL
1895 - 1952

WAS THE FIRST BLACK TO WIN A ACADEMY AWARD "OSCAR" IN 1939 FOR-THE BEST SUPPORTING ROLE - IN THE MOVIE - GONE WITH THE WIND. ALSO THE FIRST NE-GRO ACTRESS TO STAR IN A COAST TO COAST RADIO SHOW "BEULAH" IN 1947.

FROM SHOE-SHINER TO U.S. CONSUL

MIFFLIN WISTAR GIBBS

1. LAWYER AND ANTI-SLAVERY AGITATOR WHO HAD AN INTERESTING CAREER. HE OPENED THE FIRST SHOE STORE IN SAN FRANCISCO. IN 1858 GOLD WAS DISCOVERED IN BRITISH COLUMBIA, CANADA.

MUD

HE BEGAN HIS CAREER AS A SHOE-SHINE BOY IN FRISCO.

GEO LEE

3. IN LITTLE ROCK, ARK, WHERE HE HAD SETTLED. IN 1873 HE WAS ELECTED CITY JUDGE, THE FIRST BLACK TO HOLD SUCH AN OFFICE IN THE U.S. IN 1877 PRES. HAYES APPOINTED HIM U.S. REGISTRAR OF THE U.S. LAND OFFICE IN THE EASTERN DIST. OF ARK. PRESIDENT McKINLEY APPOINTED HIM U.S. CONSUL TO TAMATAVE, MADAGASCAR AN ISLAND OF E. AFRICA. (1897) HE SERVED 4 YEARS. DIED-1915.

YOU WERE DRIVING YOUR HORSES WHILE DRUNK

YOUR HONOR I COULDN'T WALK

2. HE WENT TO VICTORIA, B.C., AND OPENED A MERCHANDISE STORE. BECAME INTERESTED IN LAW AND IN 1868 RETURNED TO THE U.S. TO STUDY. HE ENTERED OBERLIN COLLEGE LAW SCHOOL AND GRADUATED IN 1870. GIBBS WAS ADMITTED TO THE BAR

19

NOTED LAWYER

D. AUGUSTUS STRAKER

BORN IN BRIDGETOWN, BARBADOS, W.I., ON JULY 11, 1842., RECEIVED HIS EARLY EDUCATION FROM HIS MOTHER. HIS PREPARATORY SCHOOLING FROM CENTRAL HIGH. BECAME A SCHOOLMASTER AT 17. WENT TO THE U.S. IN 1867 AND TAUGHT SCHOOL IN KENTUCKY IN 1869. HE ENTERED THE HOWARD U., LAW SCHOOL AS A STUDENT, GRADUATING IN 1871 WITH HONORS. SERVED AS CLERK IN THE SIXTH AUDITOR'S OFFICE OF THE U.S. TREASURY UNTIL 1875. OPENED LAW PRACTICE IN ORANGE-BURG, S.C. ELECTED 3-TIMES TO THE STATE GENERAL ASSEMBLY (S.C.)

Geo LEE

BUT WAS DENIED HIS SEAT BECAUSE HE WAS A REPUBLICAN. IN 1882 HE TAUGHT LAW AT ALLEN U., IN COLUMBIA, S.C. HE LEFT THE SOUTH IN 1887 FOR DETROIT, MICH., WHERE HE FOUND A LUCRATIVE LAW PRACTICE. HE WON THE CIVIL RIGHTS CASE OF FERGUSON vs GIES, 82nd MICH., WHICH GAVE THE NEGRO THE RIGHT TO PUBLIC ACCOMMO-DATIONS IN THAT STATE. HE ROSE TO GREAT DISTINCTION AS AN ATTORNEY. IN 1893 HE WAS ELECTED CIRCUIT COURT COMMISSIONER FOR WAYNE COUNTY. AN OUTSTANDING LEC-TURER AND A FIGHTER FOR CIVIL RIGHTS. HE WAS CHOSEN PRES., OF THE NAT'L., FEDERA-TION OF COLORED MEN IN THE U.S. IN 1895.

© 1973 George L. Lee Feature Service

MR. STRAKER WROTE A UNIQUE LAW PAMPHLET, ON THE "LARCENY OF DOGS," SHOWING CONCLUSIVELY THAT PUNISHMENT FOR STEALING DOGS CAN ONLY BE BY STATUTE, DOGS BEING AT COMMON LAW OF NO VALUE. HE ALSO WROTE THE BOOK "THE NEW SOUTH INVESTIGATED."

ACCORDING TO HISTORIANS

"VICTORY AT ADOWA"
MENELEK II

EMPEROR OF ABYSSINIA, KING OF KINGS OF ETHIOPIA. BORN SHALA MARIEM, THE SON OF THE KING OF SHOA, A PROVINCE OF ETHIOPIA IN 1844. HE CLAIMED TO BE A DIRECT DESCENDANT OF SOLOMON BY THE QUEEN OF SHEBA. HIS FATHER DIED IN 1855 AND THE THRONE WAS CLAIMED BY KASSI, THE GOVERNOR AS THEODORE III. SHALA WAS HELD PRISONER FOR 10-YEARS. HE ESCAPED AND SOUGHT REFUGE WITH QUEEN WORKITU OF WOLLO GALLAS. AIDED BY THE QUEEN HE RETURNED TO SHOA.

THEODORE III RAISED AN ARMY AGAINST HIM BUT THE SHOANS REFUSED TO FIGHT AGAINST SHALA. AFTER SEVERAL YEARS OF UNSUCCESSFUL ATTEMPTS HE WAS FINALLY ELECTED TO THE THRONE AS EMPEROR MENELEK II ON NOV 4, 1889. AT THIS TIME HE SIGNED THE TREATY OF UCCIALLI WITH ITALY, GIVING THE ITALIANS CLAIM TO THE ASMARA DISTRICT. HOWEVER ONE OF THE ARTICLES GAVE ITALY DOMINATION OVER ALL THE EMPIRE. MENELEK PROTESTED AND WENT TO WAR. DEFEATING THE ITALIANS AT AMBA ALAGI AND COMPELLED THEM TO CAPITULATE AT ADOWA IN FEB 1896. THE TREATY OF ADDIS ABABA GIVING ABSOLUTE INDEPENDENCE OF ABYSSINIA, OCT 26, 1896. MENELEK DIED 1913.

Geo LEE

TEACHER-MINISTER-BANKER

W.R. PETTIFORD

WAS BORN IN GRANVILLE COUNTY, N.C. ON JAN 20, 1847. HIS PARENTS WERE FARMERS AND BOTH FREE. THE ELDEST OF 4 CHILDREN HE HAD TO WORK ON THE FARM. LITTLE TIME FOR EDUCATION BUT THRU HARD WORK AND PERSEVERANCE FOR MANY YEARS HE QUALIFIED FOR THE MARION NORMAL SCHOOL IN ALABAMA. HE TAUGHT PRIMARY SCHOOL, BECAME A PRINCIPAL. LATER AN ASS'T TEACHER AT SELMA U., WHERE HE STUDIED THEOLOGY. IN 1879 HE BECAME A PASTOR IN A CHURCH AT UNION SPRINGS. IN 1883 HE WENT TO BIRMINGHAM TO PASTOR THE 16TH ST. BAPTIST CHURCH. HE HAD A KEEN SENSE FOR FINANCE. IN 1899 HE WAS ELECTED THE FIRST PRESIDENT OF THE ALABAMA PENNY SAVINGS+LOAN CO.

THE 'ALMORAVIDES'

A BLACK BERBER HORDE FROM THE SAHARA WHICH IN THE 11TH CENTURY FOUNDED THE FOURTH DYNASTY IN MOROCCO, IN 1055 A.D. WHEN THE MOORS OF SPAIN WERE THREATENED WITH EXPULSION BY THE WHITE CHRISTIANS FROM THE NORTH, THEY IMPLORED THE ALMORAVIDES TO AID THEM. THEY CAME AND AT THE BATTLE OF ZALLAKA IN 1086, DEFEATED THE CHRISTIAN ARMY 3-TIMES THEIR SIZE. THEY RULED SPAIN-60 YRS.

Geo. LEE

©1971. George L. Lee Feature Service

DIPLOMAT – JOURNALIST

JOSEPH C. JEREMIE

1859 – 1958

1. ONE OF HAITI'S MOST DISTINGUISHED CITIZENS WHO LIVED TO BE 99-YEARS YOUNG. IN 1882 HE FOUNDED THE FIRST NEWSPAPER EVER PRINTED IN HAITI. HE BEGAN HIS DIPLOMATIC CAREER AS AN EMBASSY CLERK. SERVED AS MINISTER OF STATE AND OF WAR AND AS A SUPREME COURT JUSTICE.

2. HIS COLORFUL LIFE HAD ITS UPS AND DOWNS; HE WAS EXILED TWICE FROM HAITI FOR HIS POLITICAL ACTIVITIES. ONCE DECORATED BY POPE PIUS XII AND WAS ONE OF THE SIGNERS OF THE CUBAN ACT OF INDEPENDENCE. ON HIS 97th BIRTHDAY HE WAS PRESENTED WITH HAITI'S HIGHEST HONOR - THE ORDRE D'HONNEUR ET MERITE - BY PRES. PAUL MAGLORIE. PERHAPS HIS

3. GREATEST HERITAGE WAS BEING THE GREAT GRANDSON OF THE FAMOUS JEAN BAPTISTE POINT DUSABLE, EXPLORER WHO FOUNDED 'CHICAGO' IN 1779. JEREMIE AN AUTHOR OF 10 BOOKS WROTE "HAITI AND CHICAGO" PUBLISHED IN FRENCH IN 1950. A RELIGIOUS MAN HE WOULD CLIMB 102-STEPS TO HIS CHURCH-AT 98!

Geo LEE

© 1971 George L. Lee Feature Service

23

RELIGIOUS PAINTER

HENRY OSSAWA TANNER
1859 – 1937

BORN IN PITTSBURGH, PA., THE SON OF BENJAMIN TUCKER TANNER WHO BECAME BISHOP OF THE AFRICAN METHODIST EPISCOPAL CHURCH IN 1888. AT AGE 13 HE DECIDED TO BECOME AN ARTIST. AFTER HIGH SCHOOL HE ENTERED THE PENNSYLVANIA ACADEMY OF THE FINE ARTS AND STUDIED UNDER THE FAMOUS THOMAS EAKINS IN PHILADELPHIA. ALSO STUDIED IN PARIS WHERE HE WENT IN 1891. HIS FIRST EXHIBIT WAS AT THE SALON IN 1895. HE WON ACCLAIM. HIS PAINTINGS GAINED WORLD RENOWN AT THE PARIS EXPOSITION IN 1900. HE WON THE GOLD MEDAL AT THE PANAMA PACIFIC EXPOSITION HELD IN SAN FRANCISCO IN 1915. HIS HONORS WERE NUMEROUS. HIS RELIGIOUS PAINTINGS BECAME FAMOUS. THE FRENCH GOVERNMENT BOUGHT HIS "RAISING OF LAZARUS" AND PLACED IT IN THE LOUVRE, THE HIGHEST HONOR GIVEN AN ARTIST IN FRANCE. HIS "THE DESTRUCTION OF SODOM AND GOMORRAH" IN THE METROPOLITAN MUSEUM (N.Y.). HE WAS A KNIGHT OF THE LEGION OF HONOUR; A MEMBER OF THE PARIS SOCIETY OF AMERICAN PAINTERS AND THE NATIONAL ACADEMY OF DESIGN (N.Y.).

MONSIEUR TANNER MAGNIFCO!

DE LAWD of GREEN PASTURES

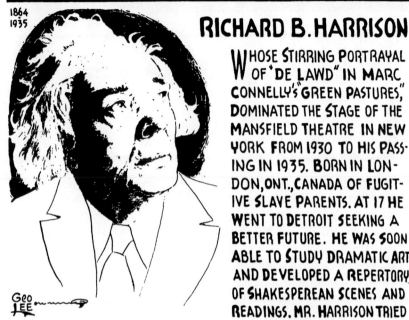

1864
1935

RICHARD B. HARRISON

WHOSE STIRRING PORTRAYAL OF "DE LAWD" IN MARC CONNELLY'S "GREEN PASTURES," DOMINATED THE STAGE OF THE MANSFIELD THEATRE IN NEW YORK FROM 1930 TO HIS PASSING IN 1935. BORN IN LONDON, ONT., CANADA OF FUGITIVE SLAVE PARENTS. AT 17 HE WENT TO DETROIT SEEKING A BETTER FUTURE. HE WAS SOON ABLE TO STUDY DRAMATIC ART AND DEVELOPED A REPERTORY OF SHAKESPEREAN SCENES AND READINGS. MR. HARRISON TRIED

Geo
LEE

TO ARRANGE RECITAL TOURS BUT NO SUCCESS. FINALLY A LYCEUM BUREAU BOOKED HIM AS A DRAMATIC READER FOR NEGRO AUDIENCES. HE STUDIED DRAMA AND TAUGHT AT A & T COLLEGE (N.C). AT 65, HE WAS PREVAILED UPON TO PLAY THE ROLE OF "DE LAWD." HIS SUCCESS WAS LATE BUT AFTER 1,657 PERFORMANCES HE ACHIEVED IMMORTALITY!

CHARLES WOOD REPLACED HARRISON AS "DE LAWD." BORN IN NASHVILLE, TENN. HE TAUGHT ENGLISH, DRAMA AND PUBLIC-SPEAKING AT TUSKEGEE INST., FLA. A & M COLLEGE, AND BENNETT COLLEGE (N.C).

25

FIRST BLACK COL. IN U.S. ARMY

COL. CHARLES YOUNG 1864 1922

A PIONEER FOR BLACKS AS OFFICERS IN THE U.S. ARMY. YOUNG ENDURED HUMILIATION BUT ROSE TO THE RANK OF COLONEL, THE FIRST BLACK TO DO SO. HE HELD THE RANK WHEN THE U.S. ENTERED WORLD WAR I IN APRIL 1917. BORN IN MAYSLICK, KY., THE SON OF A CIVIL WAR SOLDIER, HE WAS EDUCATED IN RIPLEY, OHIO. LATER TAUGHT IN THE PUBLIC SCHOOLS. IN 1884 HE WAS ADMITTED TO WEST POINT AND GRADUATED 2nd LT., ON AUG 31,

Geo LEE

DESPITE TAUNTS AND JEERS YOUNG GRAD-UATED FROM WEST POINT MILITARY ACADEMY

1889.. THE THIRD BLACK. HE SERVED IN THE 9th CALVARY REGIMENT AND 10th BOTH BLACK. HE SAW ACTION IN THE SPANISH-AMERICAN WAR— PHILIPPINES AND THE EX-PEDITION TO MEXICO TO CAPTURE PANCHO VILLA. HE WAS MILITARY ATTACHE' TO HAITI AND LIBERIA. ALTHO HE WAS IN LINE FOR BRIG. GEN., THE ARMY RETIRED HIM. HE DIED IN LAGOS, NIGERIA.

BRILLIANT EDUCATOR

DR. JOHN HOPE
1868 - 1936

BORN IN AUGUSTA, GA., ON JUNE 2. HE WAS EDUCATED AT THE WORCESTER (MASS) ACADEMY AND BROWN UNIV., WHERE HE RECEIVED A B.A. DEGREE IN 1894. HE ENTERED THE TEACHING PROFESSION AT ROGER WILLIAMS UNIV., NASHVILLE, TENN. HE TAUGHT UNTIL 1898 WHEN HE WENT TO THE ATLANTA BAPTIST COLLEGE WHICH LATER BECAME MOREHOUSE COLLEGE. IN 1906 HE WAS ELECTED PRESIDENT OF MOREHOUSE AND SERVED UNTIL 1931 WHEN HE BECAME PRES. OF ATLANTA UNIV. DR. HOPE WAS ELECTED TO THE PHI BETA KAPPA, HONOR SOCIETY IN 1919. HE RECEIVED HONORARY DOCTOR OF LAWS DEGREES FROM HOWARD U(D.C.); BATES COLLEGE (MAINE); M⁰MASTER U(TORONTO); AND BUCKNELL U(PA). DURING WORLD WAR I, HE SERVED AS A "Y" WORKER AMONG BLACK TROOPS IN FRANCE IN 1918-19. THE 8TH LIBERTY SHIP NAMED FOR A BLACK DURING WORLD WAR II WAS THE "SS JOHN HOPE" LAUNCHED ON JAN 8, 1944 AT RICHMOND, CALIF. DR. HOPE WAS ACTIVE IN CIVIL RIGHTS AND BLACK HISTORY.

Geo. LEE

LT. COMDR. EDWARD S. HOPE

THE ELDEST SON OF DR. HOPE WAS THE FIRST BLACK NAVY LT. COMMANDER IN U.S. HISTORY (1946). HE SERVED AS DIRECTOR OF INSTRUCTION AT NAVY PACIFIC UNIV., IN PEARL HARBOR. IN 1944 HE WAS THE FIRST LIEUTENANT IN THE CIVIL ENGINEERING CORPS V(S)- U.S. NAVAL RESERVE. A NATIVE OF ATLANTA, GA., HE STUDIED AT MOREHOUSE AND MASS. INSTITUTE OF TECHNOLOGY. A PH.D. FROM COLUMBIA.

BRILLIANT SCHOLAR

DR. WILLIAM EDWARD BURGHARDT DU BOIS
1868 - 1963

OUTSTANDING SCHOLAR OF HIS TIME; AUTHOR, FOREMOST SOCIAL SCIENTIST, EDUCATOR AND STATESMAN. LISTED IN WHO'S WHO IN AMERICA; FOUNDER OF THE PAN-AFRICAN CONGRESS AND THE FIRST BLACK MEMBER OF THE NAT'L INSTITUTE OF ARTS & LETTERS.

Geo LEE

2. TWO YEARS. HE RETURNED TO THE U.S. AND TOOK A POSITION AS A TEACHER AT WILBERFORCE. AFTER 2 YEARS, HE TAUGHT 1 YEAR AT THE U OF PENN. IN 1895 HE RECEIVED HIS PH.D FROM HARVARD, THE FIRST BLACK AMERICAN TO WIN THIS HONOR.

1. HE WAS BORN FEB 23 IN GREAT BARRINGTON, MASS., WHERE HE RECEIVED HIS EARLY EDUCA-TION. IN 1888 HE GRADUATED FROM FISK U. WITH A B.S. DEGREE. HE WENT TO HARVARD AND GRADUATED WITH A B.S. DEGREE IN 1890 AND AN M.A. IN 1891. NEXT TO THE UNIV. OF BERLIN FOR

3. HE BECAME PROF. OF HISTORY AND ECONOMICS AT ATLANTA U., IN 1897. HE LEFT AND WENT TO N.Y.C. IN 1910 AND HELPED TO FOUND THE NATIONAL ASSOCIATION FOR THE ADVANCEMENT OF COLORED PEOPLE

4. (NAACP). HE WAS FOUNDER AND FIRST EDITOR OF THE CRISIS MAGAZINE FOR 23 YEARS. A DYNAMIC CHAMPION OF THE RIGHTS OF HIS PEOPLE, HIS BOOK "BLACK RECONSTRUCTION" WAS A MASTERPIECE IN HISTORY AND SOCIOLOGY. HIS MANY BOOKS INCLUDE "THE SOULS OF BLACK FOLK". HE DIED IN ACCRA, GHANA.

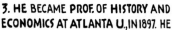

© 1977, George L. Lee Feature Service

FATHER of AFRICAN EDUCATION

DR. JAMES E.K. AGGREY
1872 - 1927

SON OF A FANTI TRIBE CHIEF WAS BORN IN ANAMABA, GOLD COAST (GHANA). THE AGGREY FAMILY ROOTS WERE 900-YEARS IN THE SOIL OF AFRICAN HISTORY. AT THE AGE OF 8 HE STUDIED AT A WHITE MISSION. AT 15 HE TAUGHT YOUNG BOYS. AT 23 HE WAS HEADMASTER OF A SCHOOL AND SECRETARY OF THE ABORIGINES RIGHTS PROTECTIVE ASSN., WHO FORCED THE DEFEAT OF AN ENGLISH BILL THAT WOULD HAVE TAKEN THE LAND FROM THE AFRICANS. HE CAME TO AMERICA AND STUDIED AT LIVINGSTONE COLLEGE IN SALISBURY, N.C., AND LATER TAUGHT THERE. HE ORGANIZED THE FIRST NEGRO CREDIT UNION IN THE U.S. WHICH HELPED THE POOR FARMERS.

AFTER 20-YEARS THE BRILLIANT ORATOR AND THINKER RETURNED TO THE GOLD COAST, A SCHOLARLY HERO. HE TAUGHT THE AFRICANS THE IMPORTANCE OF AN EDUCATION, OF NATIONALISTIC PRIDE IN THEIR RACE. HE BELIEVED IN WOMEN'S RIGHTS. HE WAS THE FIRST AFRICAN ON THE ADMIN. STAFF OF THE FAMED ACHIMOTA COLLEGE, A TEACHER TRAINING INSTITUTE ESTABLISHED JAN 28, 1927. A SCHOLAR!

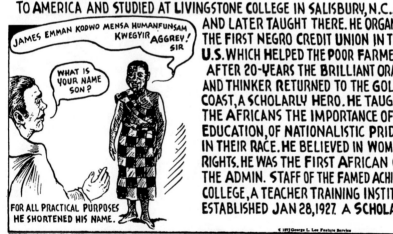

© 1973 George L. Lee Feature Service

DISWASHER · GROCER BUSINESS HEAD · BANKER !

PRESIDENT OF THE MECHANICS AND FARMERS BANK

SUCCESS STORY OF

CHARLES CLINTON SPAULDING

1874 - 1952

1. **B**ORN ON HIS FATHER'S FARM IN COLUMBUS, N.C. ON AUG 1st. THE THIRD OF A FAMILY OF FOURTEEN. AT AN EARLY AGE

2. HE WENT TO DURHAM, GETTING A JOB AS DISHWASHER AT TEN-DOLLARS A MONTH AND BOARD. LATER A BELLBOY. STUDYING NIGHTS HE GRADUATED FROM THE PUBLIC SCHOOLS.

Geo. Lee

3. YOUNG C.C. WAS GIVEN A JOB AS MANAGER OF A GROCERY. HIS BUSINESS ABILITY WAS SOON NOTICED BY OTHER

4. BUSINESS MEN-MAINLY JOHN MERRICK, A BARBER AND DR. MOORE WHO HAD ORGANIZED THE NORTH CAROLINA MUTUAL INS. CO., IN 1898. C.C. STARTED AS OFFICE BOY, AGENT, CLERK, OFFICE MANAGER AND THEN GENERAL MANAGER. IN 1923 HE BECAME PRESIDENT AND UNDER HIS LEADERSHIP

HARMON AWARD FOR DISTINGUISHED ACHIEVEMENT IN BUSINESS — 1926 — "SUCCESS IS CARVED OUT WITH THE CHISEL OF EFFICIENCY, INTEGRITY AND HARD WORK."

C.C. SPAULDING

5. IT GREW TO BECOME THE RICHEST BLACK INSURANCE CO. IN THE WORLD - IN 1899 $393.50 WAS COLLECTED - IN 1969 ASSETS WERE 98 MILLION. HE WAS PRESIDENT UNTIL 1952.

The SCHOMBURG COLLECTION

ARTHUR A. SCHOMBURG

1874 - 1938

FAMED CURATOR WAS BORN IN PUERTO RICO PARTLY OF NEGRO DESCENT. HE WAS EDUCATED IN PUERTO RICO AND IN ST. THOMAS COLLEGE. IN 1891 HE WENT TO THE U.S. AND N.Y.C. WHILE WORKING AS A CLERK AT THE BANKER'S TRUST CO., HE HAD THE BURNING DESIRE FOR KNOWLEDGE OF BLACK PEOPLE. THRU HIS EFFORTS HE FOUNDED THE "SCHOMBURG COLLECTION" THE LARGEST COLLECTION OF MATERIAL ON THE BLACK

Geo LEE

PUT THIS ONE ON THE TOP SHELF

EXPERIENCE. IN 1926 THE CARNEGIE CORP., BOUGHT THE COLLECTION AND GAVE IT TO THE HARLEM BRANCH OF THE N.Y. PUBLIC LIBRARY. BY 1970 IT HAD GROWN TO OVER 45,000 BOOKS, 4,000 MANUSCRIPTS AND PAMPHLETS. HE TRAVELED THOUSANDS OF MILES SEEKING THE BLACK MAN'S PAST!

© 1974 George L. Lee Feature Service

31

FUNNY MAN

BERT WILLIAMS
1876 - 1922

BORN IN ANTIGUA, BRITISH WEST INDIES, HE CAME TO THE **U.S.** AND CALIFORNIA AT AN EARLY AGE. HE STARTED HIS CAREER WITH JOKES AND BANJO PLAYING. LATER HE TEAMED UP WITH GEORGE WALKER AND SOON BECAME A COMEDY HIT. THEIR FAME CARRIED THEM TO NEW YORK AND ENGLAND. AFTER

WALKER DIED IN 1909, BERT JOINED THE "ZIEGFELD FOLLIES", THE FIRST BLACK. HE BECAME A SENSATION. DURING HIS TIME, BLACKFACE WAS POPULAR AND HE WAS NO EXCEPTION. A MASTER OF PANTOMIME HE WAS OFTEN CALLED THE GREATEST COMEDIAN THAT EVER LIVED – A COMEDIAN'S COMEDIAN. EDDIE CANTOR'S TRIBUTE TO BERT– "THE BEST TEACHER I EVER HAD." IN 1917 THEY PLAYED TOGETHER IN A SKIT IN THE ZIEGFELD FOLLIES. FOR OVER 20 YEARS AMERICA LAUGHED AT HIS **GENIUS.'**

Geo Lee

WILLIAM STANLEY B. BRAITHWAITE
1878 - 1962

BORN IN **BOSTON,** MASS. OF WEST INDIAN PARENTS. **SELF-EDUCATED** HE BECAME A **LITERARY CRITIC, ANTHOLOGIST** AND **POET.** WROTE HIS **FIRST** BOOK OF POEMS IN 1904. EDITED THE ANTHOLOGY OF MAGAZINE VERSE AND **YEAR BOOK** OF AMERICAN POETRY FROM 1913 TO 1929. PROF. OF **LITERATURE** AT **ATLANTA U-** 1936 TO 1945. WORKED ON THE BOSTON **TRANSCRIPT'S** LITERARY **STAFF.** WROTE MANY BOOKS.

84 HOME-RUNS IN ONE SEASON!

JOSH GIBSON,

Geo Lee

1911 - 1947

THE GREAT **CATCHER** OF THE WASHINGTON HOMESTEAD GRAYS WAS A **FABULOUS** HITTER. IN 1945 HE LED THE **NEGRO NAT'L** LEAGUE WITH A .393 AV. HE HIT THE **FIRST** HOMER EVER INTO THE LEFT-FIELD BLEACHERS IN THE YANKEE STAD.

MEDAL OF HONOR·WINNERS

WILLIAM H.THOMPKINS

A SOLDIER OF THE 10th U.S. CAVALRY. DURING THE SPANISH AMERICAN WAR WON HIS MEDAL ON JULY 1,1898. WITH THREE FELLOW SOLDIERS HE VOLUNTARILY GOT INTO AN OPEN BOAT AND UNDER HEAVY SPANISH FIRE WENT TO THE RESCUE OF WOUNDED COMRADES WHO HAD LANDED OFF THE COAST OF TAYABOCA, CUBA AND BROUGHT THEM BACK ALIVE!

GEO LEE

ROBERT PENN

A FIREMAN ON THE U.S.S. IOWA. DURING THE BATTLE OF GUANTANAMO BAY, CUBA ON JULY 20, 1898 HE RUSHED INTO THE BOILER-ROOM FROM WHICH LIVE-STEAM WAS ESCAPING IN DEADLY VOLUME AND SAVED A COAL PASSER. HE PUT OUT THE FIRE AND PREVENTED AN EXPLOSION!

1980 GEO L. LEE FEATURE SERVICE

SGT. GEORGE H. WANTON

BY THE ACT OF CONGRESS SERGEANT WANTON WAS AWARDED THE CONGRESSIONAL MEDAL OF HONOR FOR HIS EXTRAORDINARY HEROISM DURING THE SPANISH-AMERICAN WAR. ON JUNE 30, 1898 AT TAYBACOA, CUBA HE WENT VOLUNTARILY TO THE RESCUE OF HIS COMRADES. IN AN OPEN BOAT UNDER FIRE OF SPANISH CANNONS HE REACHED THE SHORE AND BROUGHT THEM BACK SAFELY. SGT. WANTON WAS ONE OF THE PALL-BEARERS OF THE UNKNOWN SOLDIER. A NATIVE OF FALL RIVER, R.I., HE JOINED THE 10TH CALVARY.

Geo Lee

DR. EMMETT J. SCOTT

COMING! MR. WASHINGTON

SECRETARY TO THE GREAT EDUCATOR, BOOKER T. WASHINGTON FOR 20-YEARS, WAS AN OUTSTANDING PERSONALITY. IN 1909 HE WAS APPOINTED A MEMBER OF THE AMERICAN COMM. TO LIBERIA BY PRES. WM H. TAFT; SEC'Y NAT'L NEGRO BUSINESS LEAGUE (1900-1922); SPECIAL ASS'T TO THE SECRETARY OF WAR 1917-1919; SEC'Y-TREAS-BUS., MGR HOWARD U., 1919-1938; MEMBER PAROLE BOARD FOR D.C., 1932-39; DIRECTOR OF PERSONNEL, No.4 YARD OF THE SUN SHIPBUILDING CO-AT THE AGE 73. (1946)

© 1973 George L. Lee Feature Service

35

SIDNEY LOMAN - SCOUTING AT 100

THE WORLD'S OLDEST ACTIVE SCOUT-MASTER AT AGE 100 (1980). LEADER OF HIS BOY SCOUT TROOP 420 OF THE BETHEL A.M.E. CHURCH IN SAN DIEGO. BORN NEAR WACO, TEX., OF A BLACK FATHER AND A CREEK INDIAN MOTHER. HE ORGANIZED HIS FIRST BLACK TROOP IN IMPERIAL VALLEY (CAL) IN 1921 AND IN SAN DIEGO (1941). NEARLY 9,000 SCOUTS HAVE BEEN GUIDED BY THIS REMARKABLE MAN WHO LOST BOTH LEGS AT AGE 90...BUT CONTINUES TO LEAD FROM HIS WHEELCHAIR.

DIED 1981

FIRST BLACK MARINE GENERAL

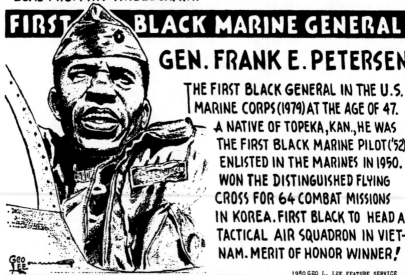

GEN. FRANK E. PETERSEN

THE FIRST BLACK GENERAL IN THE U.S. MARINE CORPS (1979) AT THE AGE OF 47. A NATIVE OF TOPEKA, KAN., HE WAS THE FIRST BLACK MARINE PILOT ('52). ENLISTED IN THE MARINES IN 1950. WON THE DISTINGUISHED FLYING CROSS FOR 64 COMBAT MISSIONS IN KOREA. FIRST BLACK TO HEAD A TACTICAL AIR SQUADRON IN VIET-NAM. MERIT OF HONOR WINNER!

1881 1952 "HELLO BILL"

J. FINLEY WILSON

GRAND EXALTED RULER OF THE "ELKS" FOR OVER 30-YEARS, HAD A VERY COLORFUL LIFE. BORN IN NASHVILLE, TENN., THE SON OF A PREACHER WHO HAD FOUGHT IN THE CIVIL WAR. HE ATTENDED FISK AND ALLEN COLLEGE. AT 15 HE WORKED ON A STAGE-COACH...BELLHOPPED IN KANSAS CITY... JOINED THE 23RD KANSAS DIVISION DURING THE SPANISH-AMERICAN WAR AND WENT TO CUBA. WAS A PULLMAN PORTER ...TOOK PART IN THE KLONDIKE GOLD RUSH ... A MINER IN ARIZONA... A COWBOY IN WYOMING. WENT TO NYC AND BECAME A NEWSPAPER REPORTER ON THE N.Y. AGE... ESTABLISHED 3-PAPERS...RAN FOR THE N.Y. STATE SENATE (23RD DIST.) IN 1946 – BUT LOST!

MISTY ERROLL GARNER
BORN IN PITTSBURGH, PA.,

INTERNATIONALLY FAMOUS JAZZ PIANIST, COMPOSER AND IMPRESSIONIST WHO WROTE "MISTY","GASLIGHT"AND"DREAMY"AMONG HIS MANY-NEVER LEARNED TO READ MUSIC! HE BEGAN PLAYING AT 3. PLAYED WITH THE "CANDY KIDS"ON RADIO AT 7. PLAYED ON RIVER-BOATS ON THE ALLEGHENY RIVER BY 11. AS A TEENAGER LEFT PITTSBURGH FOR N.Y.'S FAMED 52nd JAZZ DENS...FAME FOLLOWED. RECORDED "MISTY" WITH MITCH MILLER'S ORCH, IN 1956. HIS COMPOSITIONS WON EVERY JAZZ AWARD IN MUSICAL HISTORY. THE BRILLIANT PIANIST DIED AT 53.

**1883
1966**

HISTORIAN

JOEL A. ROGERS

BETTER KNOWN AS "J.A." WAS A SELF-MADE HISTORIAN WHOSE ACCOUNTS OF BLACK ACHIEVEMENTS HAVE BEEN REGARDED AS LEGENDS. BORN IN JAMAICA, BWI. HE DIED IN N.Y.C. HE WENT TO THE U.S. IN 1906 AND BECAME A NATURALIZED CITIZEN IN 1917. JOINED THE PITTSBURGH COURIER AS A REPORTER IN 1921 AND HE WROTE A COLUMN ON NEGRO HISTORY UNTIL HIS DEATH. HE TRAVELED EXTENSIVELY TO AFRICA AND EUROPE GATHERING STARTLING FACTS ABOUT FAMOUS WHITE PEOPLE LINKING THEM WITH BLACK KIN... AND THE BLACK MAN'S PAST. IN 1935 WHEN MUSSOLINI'S ITALIAN FASCISTS INVADED ETHIOPIA THE COURIER SENT J.A. TO COVER THE WAR. HE WAS THE FIRST BLACK WAR CORRESPONDENT. HE WROTE BOOKS BUT PUBLISHERS REFUSED TO CONSIDER HIS WORKS. IT WAS SAID, HE DESTROYED ALL OF THEIR MYTHS AND CONCEPTS. HIS FIRST BOOK..."SUPERMAN TO MAN" ALSO "SEX AND RACE", "AFRICA'S GIFT TO AMERICA" AMONG THEM. SOME WERE USED AS REFERENCE IN MAJOR UNIVERSITIES AND LIBRARIES THROUGHOUT THE WORLD. W.E.B. DuBOIS SAID OF HIM..."NO MAN LIVING HAS REVEALED SO MANY IMPORTANT FACTS ABOUT THE NEGRO RACE AS ROGERS"... TRULY AN HISTORIAN!

Geo
LEE

1984 Geo L. Lee Feature Service

♫ ♪AS TIME GOES BY♫♪

ARTHUR DOOLEY WILSON
1886-1953

THE YOUNGEST SON OF A POOR LABORER WAS BORN IN TYLER,TEXAS. HE BEGAN HIS CAREER AT SEVEN,SINGING FOR FIVE DOLLARS A WEEK AND CAKES. BY EIGHT HE WAS MAKING EIGHTEEN AND CAKES. DURING HIS YOUTH HE PLAYED MINSTREL SHOWS. HE PLAYED IRISH ROLES IN "WHITE FACE". SINGING A SONG NAMED-MR.DOOLEY - HE ACQUIRED HIS NICKNAME "DOOLEY." PLAYING DRUMS AT THE "SONTAG" IN HARLEM HE MET A YOUNG SONG WRITER-IRVING BERLIN WHO WOULD SLIP HIM 5 OR 10 TO PLUG A SONG-ALEXANDER'S RAGTIME BAND. DOOLEY SPENT MANY YEARS IN EUROPE.IN THE 1920'S HE RETURNED TO THE U.S. AND ACTED IN STOCK COMPANIES. IN "CABIN IN THE SKY" WITH ETHEL WATERS, HE CREATED THE ROLE OF-LITTLE JOE. AT 59 HE WAS SIGNED TO PLAY "SAM" IN THE MOVIE "CASABLANCA," WITH HUMPHREY BOGART, A SMALL PART. FORTUNE SMILED AND HE STOLE THE SHOW WHEN HE SANG AND PLAYED AN OLD TORCH SONG- AS TIME GOES BY- TO THE TOP OF THE HIT PARADE. ACTUALLY HE COULDN'T PLAY A NOTE!

MARY CHURCH TERRELL

THE FIRST NEGRO WOMAN IN THE U.S. TO SERVE ON A BOARD OF EDUCATION. SHE WAS A MEMBER OF THE WASH. D.C. FOR 11-YEARS. A GREAT CIVIC LEADER SHE WAS THE FIRST PRESIDENT OF THE NAT'L ASSOC. OF COLORED WOMEN.

Mr. POLITICIAN

CONG. WILLIAM L. DAWSON
1886 - 1970

BORN IN ALBANY, GA. EDUCATED AT THE ALBANY NORMAL SCHOOL AND A MAGNA CUM LAUDE GRADUATE OF FISK UNIV. DURING WORLD WAR I HE SERVED AS A FIRST LIEUTENANT IN THE 365th INFANTRY. HE WAS GASSED AND WOUNDED IN THE BATTLE AT MEUSE-ARGONNE IN FRANCE. AFTER THE WAR HE WORKED HIS WAY THRU THE NORTHWESTERN LAW SCHOOL IN EVANSTON, ILL. HE DECIDED TO ENTER CHICAGO POLITICS AND JOINED THE REPUBLICAN PARTY. IN 1928 HE MADE HIS FIRST BID FOR CONGRESS AND LOST ALSO IN 1938. HE SWITCHED TO THE DEMOCRATS IN 1939 AND BECAME WARD COMMITTEEMAN OF THE 2nd WARD. IN 1942 HE WENT TO WASHINGTON AS THE U.S. CONGRESSMAN FROM THE FIRST DIST. OF ILL., ONE OF THE RICHEST IN THE U.S. AND STAYED UNTIL HIS DEATH IN 1970. HE WAS SEC'Y OF THE DEMOCRATIC CONGRESSIONAL COMM., IN 1944-46-48: FIRST BLACK CHAIRMAN OF A HOUSE COMMITTEE-ON EXPENDITURES: CHAIRMAN OF THE HOUSE GOV'T OPERATIONS COMM., AND VICE-CHAIRMAN OF THE DEMOCRATIC NAT'L COMMITTEE.

Geo LEE

* 1972 George L. Lee Feature Service

BACK-TO-AFRICA

MARCUS GARVEY
1887 – 1940

1. SELF-EDUCATED, WHO WORKED AS A PRINTER, TIMEKEEPER, A NEWS-PAPERMAN IN PANAMA AND A MAGAZINE WRITER IN LONDON— BECAME A CRUSADER AND ORGANIZED OVER 3 MILLION BLACKS IN THE FIRST PRO-AFRICAN MOVEMENT IN THE U.S.

2. BORN IN JAMAICA, W.I. IN 1914 AT THE AGE OF 27 HE FOUNDED THE UNIVERSAL NEGRO IMPROVEMENT ASSN., (UNIA). IN 1916 HE CAME TO THE U.S. AND HARLEM. HE FOUNDED"THE NEGRO WORLD", NEWSPAPER. HIS ORGANIZATION BOOMED. FOUNDED AN AFRICAN ORTHODOX CHURCH. IN 1919 HE ORGANIZED THE "BLACK STAR STEAMSHIP LINE." PREACHING BLACK PRIDE HE CAPTURED THE IMAGINATION OF THOUSANDS OF

3. NEGROES. AN EARLY BLACK NATIONALIST, HE DECLARED THE REPUBLIC OF AFRICA AND BECAME ITS "PROVINCIAL PRESIDENT." HE HAD HIS OWN ARMY. HOWEVER HE RAN INTO DIFFICULTIES WITH THE U.S. AUTHORITIES ON MAIL FRAUD AND WAS DEPORTED IN 1927. A COLORFUL MAN, HE WAS SENT BACK TO HIS NATIVE JAMAICA. HE DIED IN LONDON IN 1940.

© 1971 George L. Lee Feature Service

41

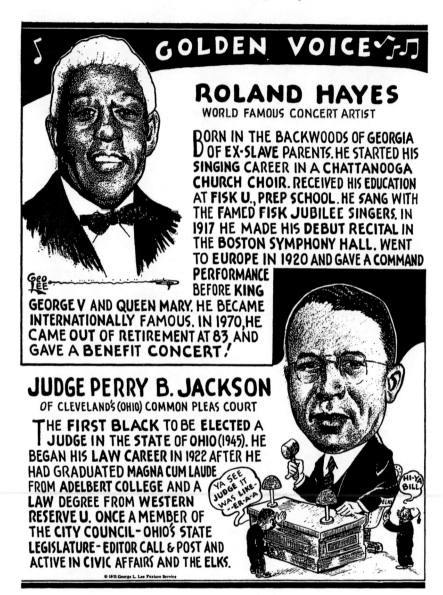

GOLDEN VOICE

ROLAND HAYES
WORLD FAMOUS CONCERT ARTIST

BORN IN THE BACKWOODS OF GEORGIA OF EX-SLAVE PARENTS. HE STARTED HIS SINGING CAREER IN A CHATTANOOGA CHURCH CHOIR. RECEIVED HIS EDUCATION AT FISK U., PREP SCHOOL. HE SANG WITH THE FAMED FISK JUBILEE SINGERS. IN 1917 HE MADE HIS DEBUT RECITAL IN THE BOSTON SYMPHONY HALL. WENT TO EUROPE IN 1920 AND GAVE A COMMAND PERFORMANCE BEFORE KING GEORGE V AND QUEEN MARY. HE BECAME INTERNATIONALLY FAMOUS. IN 1970, HE CAME OUT OF RETIREMENT AT 83, AND GAVE A BENEFIT CONCERT!

JUDGE PERRY B. JACKSON
OF CLEVELAND'S (OHIO) COMMON PLEAS COURT

THE FIRST BLACK TO BE ELECTED A JUDGE IN THE STATE OF OHIO (1945). HE BEGAN HIS LAW CAREER IN 1922 AFTER HE HAD GRADUATED MAGNA CUM LAUDE FROM ADELBERT COLLEGE AND A LAW DEGREE FROM WESTERN RESERVE U. ONCE A MEMBER OF THE CITY COUNCIL—OHIO'S STATE LEGISLATURE—EDITOR CALL & POST AND ACTIVE IN CIVIC AFFAIRS AND THE ELKS.

© 1971 George L. Lee Feature Service

KINGFISH

1887
•
1958

TIM MOORE

ONE OF THE WORLD'S FUNNIEST MEN, SPENT 60-YEARS IN SHOW BUSINESS.

BORN IN ROCK ISLAND, ILL., TIM HAD A FLARE FOR SHO-BIZ AT AN EARLY AGE. AT 11, WAS DANCING FOR PENNIES OUTSIDE BALLPARKS -A TRAVELING VAUDEVILLE STAR AT 12-A MEDICINE SHOW CON-ARTIST AT 14 - A JOCKEY AT 15-AND A GOOD PRIZE FIGHTER AT 17, WHO FOUGHT IN ENGLAND AND AUSTRALIA UNDER THE NAME OF "YOUNG KLONDIKE." HIS SHOWMAN CAREER START-ED AROUND 1906. PLAYED BROADWAY, TOURED

NOW SAPPHIRE MY DARLIN' I CAN EXPLAIN

START TALKING

EUROPE WITH THE BLACKBIRDS REVUE. HIS BIG SUCCESS WHEN HE PLAYED "KINGFISH" IN THE TV-SHOW...AMOS AND ANDY. HIS ANTICS WERE A RIOT. A GREAT SHOWMAN!

Geo. LEE

© 1975 George L. Lee Feature Service

HORACE PIPPIN

1888
1946

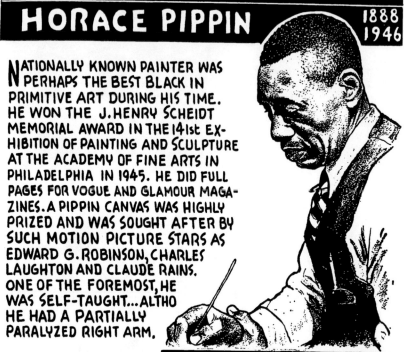

NATIONALLY KNOWN PAINTER WAS PERHAPS THE BEST BLACK IN PRIMITIVE ART DURING HIS TIME. HE WON THE J. HENRY SCHEIDT MEMORIAL AWARD IN THE 141st EXHIBITION OF PAINTING AND SCULPTURE AT THE ACADEMY OF FINE ARTS IN PHILADELPHIA IN 1945. HE DID FULL PAGES FOR VOGUE AND GLAMOUR MAGAZINES. A PIPPIN CANVAS WAS HIGHLY PRIZED AND WAS SOUGHT AFTER BY SUCH MOTION PICTURE STARS AS EDWARD G. ROBINSON, CHARLES LAUGHTON AND CLAUDE RAINS. ONE OF THE FOREMOST, HE WAS SELF-TAUGHT...ALTHO HE HAD A PARTIALLY PARALYZED RIGHT ARM.

THE 369th SERVED UNDER THE FRENCH COMMAND AND WAS

CITED FOR ITS HEROISM. THEY WERE THE FIRST U.S. BLACK TROOPS TO SEE ACTION.

A SNIPER'S BULLET CAUSED THE INJURY, WHILE SERVING WITH THE 369th INFANTRY OF N.Y., (1918) DURING WORLD WAR I, IN FRANCE. THE FRENCH AWARDED HIM WITH THE CROIX DE GUERRE FOR HEROISM. AFTER THE WAR HE HAD A GREAT URGE TO PAINT...EVEN THO DISABLED HE WOULD USE HIS LEFT HAND TO SUPPORT HIS RIGHT. A NATIVE OF WEST CHESTER, PA.

© 1976 George L. Lee Feature Serv...

♫ HIT SONG, WRITER ♪

NOBLE SISSLE 1889-1975

FAMOUS ENTERTAINER, STARTED HIS CAREER IN DAYS OF VAUDEVILLE. A PROLIFIC WRITER OF HIT SONGS, A GIFTED TENOR. BORN IN INDIANAPOLIS, IND., THE SON OF A MINISTER AND A MOTHER WHO WANTED HIM TO BE A SINGING EVANGELIST. HIS FATHER DIED WHILE HE WAS IN BUTLER U., AND HE HAD TO DROPOUT TO SUPPORT THE FAMILY. HE GOT A SINGING JOB WITH JIM EUROPE'S DANCE BAND IN BALTIMORE. EUBIE BLAKE PLAYED THE PIANO. WORLD WAR I CAME ALONG AND EUROPE HEADED THE 369th ALL-BLACK

"YOU WERE MEANT FOR ME."
"LOVE WILL FIND A WAY."

SISSLE AND BLAKE FIRST MET IN 1915 AND CONTINUED AS A TEAM IN VAUDEVILLE AND MUSIC FOR A LIFETIME.

"MIRANDA."
"BANDANA DAYS."
"I'M JUST WILD ABOUT HARRY."
"SWANEE MOON."
"ALONE WITH LOVE."
"GYPSY BLUES."

NOBLE WROTE THE WORDS, EUBIE THE MUSIC OF 'SHUFFLE ALONG' AND 'CHOCOLATE DANDIES' DURING THE 1920's.

INFANTRY BAND. SISSLE WENT ALONG AS DRUM MAJOR SGT., AND ENTERTAINED THE SOLDIERS IN FRANCE. AFTER THE WAR WHILE TOURING THE NATION WITH BLAKE THEY MET THE COMEDY TEAM, MILLER AND LYLES "AND TOGETHER THEY CONCEIVED....
"SHUFFLE ALONG."(1921). PLAYED BROADWAY FOR 2-YEARS. ACTIVE IN THE USO SHOWS, DURING WORLD WAR II. FOUNDER AND FIRST PRESIDENT OF THE NEGRO ACTORS GUILD. 1987 GEO L. LEE FEATURE SERVICE

Madame Evanti

THE FIRST FAMOUS BLACK OPERA SINGER, LILLIAN EVANS TIBBS WAS BORN IN WASH, D.C. AFTER HER MUSICAL STUDIES AT HOWARD UNIV., AND FURTHER STUDY IN EUROPE, SHE MADE HER DEBUT IN NICE, FRANCE IN 1925 IN THE OPERA "LAKME". SHE TOURED THE OPERA HOUSES IN ITALY...GAVE CONCERTS IN GERMANY. IN 1932 THE METROPOLITAN OPERA CO. REFUSED TO LET HER SING. BUT SHE GAVE CONCERTS THROUGHOUT THE U.S. AIDED IN THE FOUNDING OF THE NEGRO NAT'L OPERA CO. A GOOD-WILL AMBASSADOR FOR THE STATE DEPT. TO LATIN AMERICA AND PERFORMING WITH TOSCANINI AND THE NBC ORCHESTRA IN 1940s-50s. WROTE "SALUTE TO GHANA" FOR VOICE OF AMERICA. (1957)

1890
1967

Geo Lee

SOCIOLOGIST E. FRANKLIN FRAZIER PH.D

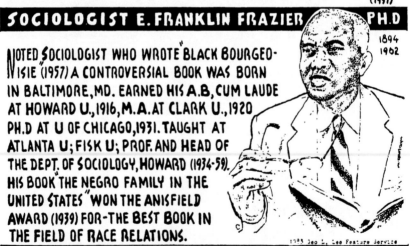

1894
1962

NOTED SOCIOLOGIST WHO WROTE "BLACK BOURGEOISIE" (1957) A CONTROVERSIAL BOOK WAS BORN IN BALTIMORE, MD. EARNED HIS A.B, CUM LAUDE AT HOWARD U., 1916, M.A. AT CLARK U., 1920 PH.D AT U OF CHICAGO, 1931. TAUGHT AT ATLANTA U; FISK U; PROF. AND HEAD OF THE DEPT. OF SOCIOLOGY, HOWARD (1934-59). HIS BOOK "THE NEGRO FAMILY IN THE UNITED STATES" WON THE ANISFIELD AWARD (1939) FOR-THE BEST BOOK IN THE FIELD OF RACE RELATIONS.

1993 Geo L. Lee Feature Service

BURNING SPEAR

JOMO KENYATTA

PRES., OF KENYA, AFRICA. BORN IN 1890 OF PEASANT PARENTS OF THE KIKUYU TRIBE. ONCE A HUNTER KNOWN AS "BURNING SPEAR."

Geo LEE

1. BAPTIZED AS JOHNSTONE KAMAU. IN HIS YOUTH HE WORE A WIDE ORNAMENTAL BELT CALLED A KENYATTA. JOMO MEANS BURNING SPEAR. HIS GRANDFATHER WAS A GOOD WITCH DOCTOR. EARLY EDUCATION IN THE MISSION SCHOOLS OF THE CHURCH OF SCOTLAND. AFTER THE COLONIAL CONQUEST, THE BRITISH OPENED THE DOOR TO WHITE SETTLERS TO FARM THE RICH HIGHLANDS OF KENYA. THEY TOOK OVER AND RULED. KENYATTA BECAME INTERESTED IN POLITICS AND SOUGHT TO RESTORE THE WHITE-HELD LAND TO THE KIKUYU TRIBE. IN 1928 HE FOUNDED A JOURNAL CALLED – MUIGWITHANIA (TO UNITE).

2. IN 1931 HE WENT TO LONDON AS A SPOKESMAN FOR HIS PEOPLE AND STAYED 16 YEARS. STUDIED AT THE LONDON SCHOOL OF ECONOMICS AND WROTE FOR THE BRITISH DAILY WORKER. VISITED RUSSIA. RETURNED TO KENYA IN 1947 AND BECAME PRESIDENT OF THE KENYA AFRICA UNION. HE WAS LINKED TO THE TERRORIST GROUP CALLED **MAU MAU** WHOSE ORIGINAL PURPOSE WAS FOR AFRICANS TO REFUSE TO SELL LAND TO EUROPEANS. IN 1952 HE WAS IMPRISONED FOR THE ACTIVITIES OF THE MAU MAU. WHILE IN JAIL HE BECAME A HERO. RELEASED IN 1961 HE RETURNED HOME AND BECAME PRIME MINISTER IN 1963. SIX MONTHS LATER, KENYA WAS GRANTED FULL INDEPENDENCE (1964) – AT LAST... UHURU (FREEDOM).

CAPT. ADRIAN RICHARDSON

BORN IN PHILLISBURG, ST. MARTIN, DUTCH W. INDIES. ORPHANED AT 4, HE WAS ADOPTED BY A WHITE SEA CAPTAIN, A. C. CHENEY OF CAMBRIDGE, MASS. HIS SEA CAREER STARTED EARLY. A CABIN BOY AT 10; A MATE'S LICENSE AT 16; HIS FIRST MASTER'S LICENSE AT 18; A FULL FLEDGED CAPTAIN AT 23. DURING WORLD WAR I WAS CAPTAIN OF A U.S. TROOP TRANSPORT. ENTERED THE MERCHANT MARINE SERVICE IN AUG. 1942. HE BECAME SKIPPER OF THE LIBERTY SHIP, "S.S. FREDERICK DOUGLASS" IN MAY 1943. AFTER 6 SUCCESSFUL ATLANTIC CROSSINGS IT WAS TORPEDOED BY THE NAZIS ON SEPT. 20th. THE SHIP WAS SUNK BUT HIS MIXED CREW WERE SAVED. HE CONTINUED WORLD WAR II ON THE "S.S. ROBERT LOWERY" AND "S.S. JOHN T. MERRICK" UNTIL APRIL 1945 WHEN HE WAS STRICKEN WITH PNEUMONIA IN ANTWERP, BELGIUM. HE DIED AT 53 IN N.Y.C... NOV. 1945.

Geo LEE

DR. CHARLES S. JOHNSON
1893 - 1956

FIRST BLACK PRESIDENT OF FISK U.(1946). BORN IN BRISTOL, VA., SON OF A BAPTIST MINISTER. EDUCATED AT WAVELAND ACADEMY. AN A.B. FROM VIRGINIA UNION IN 1917. A BACHELOR OF PHILOSOPHY FROM THE UNIV. OF CHICAGO. HEAD OF THE SOCIAL SCIENCES AT FISK FOR 18 YEARS. A NOTED EDITOR AND A PROLIFIC WRITER - 18 BOOKS - THE BEST KNOWN "THE NEGRO COLLEGE GRADUATE."

Geo LEE

SAMUEL COLERIDGE-TAYLOR
1875 - 1912

BORN IN LONDON, ENGLAND. THE SON OF AN AFRICAN FATHER AND AN ENGLISH MOTHER. A BRILLIANT MUSICAL GENIUS-STUDIED THE VIOLIN AT 6. SANG WITH THE CHOIR OF ST. GEORGE'S AT 10. BECAME A COMPOSER AND CONDUCTOR. IN 1898 HIS "HIAWATHA TRILOGY" COMPOSITION MADE HIM WORLD FAMOUS. HIS SERIOUS COMPOSITIONS WERE OVER 100.

FIRST **BLACK FIGHTER** PILOT

EUGENE JACQUES BULLARD
1894 - 1961

BORN IN COLUMBUS, GA. HE ESCAPED A MOB AND RAN OFF TO EUROPE. BECAME A BOXER AT 17-JOINED THE FRENCH FOREIGN LEGION AT 19. A PILOT IN THE FAMED LAFAYETTE ESCADRILLE IN WORLD WAR I. AWARDED THE CROIX DE GUERRE, FRANCE'S HIGHEST HONOR. THE U.S. HAD NO NEGRO PILOTS IN WORLD WAR I.

JAMES A. BLAND
1854 - 1911

COMPOSER OF THE IMMORTAL SONG "CARRY ME BACK TO OLD VIRGINNY" THE OFFICIAL SONG OF THE STATE OF VIRGINIA SINCE 1940 - WAS NOT BORN IN VA., BUT IN LONG ISLAND, N.Y. HE WROTE OVER 600 SONGS INCLUDING: "IN THE EVENING BY THE MOONLIGHT" AND "OH 'DEM GOLDEN SLIPPERS."

50

BRILLIANT CHEMIST

LLOYD A. HALL
1894 - 1971

OUTSTANDING IN HIS FIELD. HE HELD OVER 100 CHEMICAL PATENTS, U.S. AND FOREIGN. HE HAS BEEN LISTED IN - WHO'S WHO IN CHEMISTRY; WHO'S WHO OF AMERICAN MEN OF SCIENCE; WHO'S WHO OF THE WEST AND WHO'S WHO IN AMERICA.

GUSH! BEEN IN EVERY BOOK

Geo Lee

1. DR. HALL WAS BORN IN ELGIN, ILL. HE RECEIVED HIS HIGHER EDUCATION AT NORTH-WESTERN U; U OF CHICAGO; TUSKEGEE; VA. STATE AND HOWARD.

2. STARTED HIS GREAT CAREER IN CHICAGO, WITH THE DEPT OF HEALTH. FROM CHEMIST TO TECHNICAL DIR., OF THE GRIFFITH LAB. (36 YEARS) HE ACHIEVED NOTABLE SUCCESS IN THE PRESERVATION OF FOOD PRODUCTS, MEAT AND BIOLOGICAL CHEMISTRY. THE UNITED NATIONS NAMED HIM A FOOD CONSULTANT TO INDONESIA IN 1961. HE WAS VERY ACTIVE IN CIVIC AFFAIRS

3. DURING HIS MANY YEARS IN CHICAGO. HE WENT TO PASADENA WHERE HE BECAME CONSULTANT FOR 5 CHEMICAL FIRMS. HE WAS A MEMBER OF THE PASADENA CHAMBER OF COMMERCE. HIS NUMEROUS HONORS WERE TREMENDOUS. HE WAS THE FIRST BLACK IN THE AMERICAN INSTITUTE OF CHEMISTS.

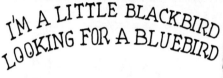

I'M A LITTLE BLACKBIRD LOOKING FOR A BLUEBIRD

FLORENCE MILLS
1895 - 1927

BORN IN WASH, D.C., SHE STARTED HER CAREER AS AN ENTERTAINER AT THE AGE OF 6, WHEN SHE APPEARED IN PRIVATE RECITALS FOR MEMBERS OF THE DIPLOMATIC CORPS. HER SKILL IN DANCING AND SINGING WAS AMAZING. SHE TOURED IN A SISTER ACT IN VAUDEVILLE, WORKED IN A CABARET IN HARLEM. IN 1921 SHE MADE HER FIRST BROADWAY APPEARANCE IN "SHUFFLE ALONG." LATER JOINED LEW LESLIE'S "PLANTATION REVUE" AND BECAME A STAR. THE SHOW TOURED LONDON UNDER THE NAME OF "DIXIE TO DOVER". ACCLAIMED AS A GIFTED ENTERTAINER SHE APPEARED IN THE NEW REVUE "BLACKBIRDS," IN 1926, SINGING THE BIG SONG "I'M A LITTLE BLACKBIRD, LOOKING FOR A BLUEBIRD." A HIT IN NEW YORK THE SHOW TOURED EUROPE. FLORENCE A SMASHING SUCCESS WAS MAKING FUTURE PLANS WHEN SHE DIED FROM AN OPERATION.

BUTTERBEANS AND SUSIE

THE FAMOUS COMEDY TEAM OF YESTERYEAR WAS THE OLDEST KNOWN ACT IN SHOW BUSINESS. THEIR SUSPICIOUS WIFE – HAPLESS HUSBAND ROUTINE WAS A RIOT. THEY STARTED IN 1917 AND LASTED UNTIL THE '50s... THEIR REAL NAMES

JODIE AND SUSIE EDWARDS

© 1993 George L. Lee Feature Service

MAN OF THE PEOPLE

WILLIAM V.S. TUBMAN

1895 - 1971

BECAME PRESIDENT OF LIBERIA ON JAN 3, 1944. LIBERIA WAS FOUNDED IN 1822 BY FREED AMERICAN SLAVES ON LAND PURCHASED BY THE WHITE-ORGANIZED AMERICAN COLON-IALIZATION SOCIETY FROM LOCAL AFRICAN CHIEFS. IT BECAME AN INDEPEND-ENT REPUBLIC IN 1847. KNOWN AS "UNCLE SHAD", HE WAS A DESCENDANT OF BLACKS FROM GEORGIA. BORN IN HARPER, LIBERIA THE SON OF A METHODIST

Geo LEE

TUBMAN SERVED WEST AFRICA'S REPUBLIC FOR 27 YEARS.

LIBERIA

MINISTER. EDUCATED AT CUTT-INGTON COLLEGE AND DIVINITY SCHOOL. A SCHOOL TEACHER, LAWYER AND SENATOR AT 28. HIS "OPEN DOOR" POLICY MADE HIM A NATIONAL HERO. HE WAS THE FIRST AFRICAN TO INVITE BLACK ENVOYS.

© 1975 George L. Lee Feature Service

53

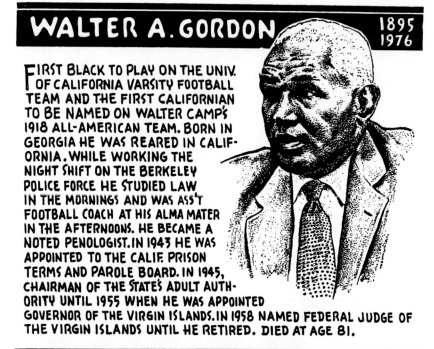

WALTER A. GORDON
1895 1976

FIRST BLACK TO PLAY ON THE UNIV. OF CALIFORNIA VARSITY FOOTBALL TEAM AND THE FIRST CALIFORNIAN TO BE NAMED ON WALTER CAMP'S 1918 ALL-AMERICAN TEAM. BORN IN GEORGIA HE WAS REARED IN CALIF-ORNIA. WHILE WORKING THE NIGHT SHIFT ON THE BERKELEY POLICE FORCE HE STUDIED LAW IN THE MORNINGS AND WAS ASS'T FOOTBALL COACH AT HIS ALMA MATER IN THE AFTERNOONS. HE BECAME A NOTED PENOLOGIST. IN 1943 HE WAS APPOINTED TO THE CALIF. PRISON TERMS AND PAROLE BOARD. IN 1945, CHAIRMAN OF THE STATE'S ADULT AUTH-ORITY UNTIL 1955 WHEN HE WAS APPOINTED GOVERNOR OF THE VIRGIN ISLANDS. IN 1958 NAMED FEDERAL JUDGE OF THE VIRGIN ISLANDS UNTIL HE RETIRED. DIED AT AGE 81.

BRICKTOP ADA SMITH DU CONGE

CAFE SOCIETY'S LIVING LEGEND WHO ENTERTAINED ROYALTY AND HI-SOCIETY IN PARIS AND ROME. COLE PORTER THE COMPOSER WROTE HER A SONG, "MISS OTIS REGRETS". BORN IN ALDERSON, W.VA., THE FRECKLED REDHEAD GOT HER SINGING AND DANCIN' START IN CHICAGO. IN 1924 SHE WENT TO PARIS FOR 6-MOS., AND STAYED 40-YRS. AT 82-PLUS, STILL... SINGS FOR SOCIETY IN N.Y. AND CHICAGO!

GEO LEE

BISHOP BRAVID W. HARRIS
1896 - 1965

FIRST BLACK BISHOP IN THE EPISCO-PAL CHURCH. BORN IN WARRENTON, N.C., HE WAS EDUCATED AT ST. AUGUS-TINE COLLEGE IN RALEIGH, N.C., AND THE BISHOP PAYNE DIVINITY SCHOOL, PETERSBURG, VA. CONSECRATED IN 1945, HE BECAME BISHOP OF LIBERIA THE OLDEST EPISCOPAL MISSION IN AFRICA. AFTER SERVING FOR 20-YEARS HE RETIRED AND BECAME ACTING DIRECTOR OF THE FOUNDATION FOR EPISCOPAL COLLEGE, THE POSITION HELD AT THE TIME OF HIS DEATH.

Geo Lee

A NAVY FIRST

LT. CLARENCE SAMUELS

THE FIRST BLACK COMMISSIONED OFFICER IN THE NAVY IN 1943, SERVING IN THE COAST GUARD. THE FIRST BLACK TO COMMAND A NAVY VESSEL WITH A MIXED CREW IN THE MODERN DAY NAVY. HE HAD SERVED FOR 23-YEARS IN NEARLY EVERY GRADE, STARTING AS A SECOND CLASS SEAMAN. HE WON RIBBONS FOR PRE-PEARL HARBOR SERVICE; PEARL HARBOR ACTION; AMERICAN THEATRE OF WAR ACTION AND AFRICAN MID-EASTERN CAMPAIGN.

THE BLACK EAGLE

COL. HUBERT FAUNTLEROY JULIAN

SOLDIER OF FORTUNE, STUNT FLYER, GUN RUNNER, MERCENARY, RUM RUNNER AND COLORFUL ADVENTURER. BORN IN TRINIDAD, BWI (1897), HE MADE HIS HOME IN NEW YORK'S HARLEM. HIS JAMES BOND CAREER STARTED IN 1923 WHEN HE PARACHUTED OVER HARLEM AND LANDED ON THE ROOF OF A BUILDING. HIS STUNT FLYING EARNED HIM THE TITLE "THE BLACK EAGLE". DURING PROHIBITION WAS AN AERIAL RUM RUNNER. PERSONAL PILOT FOR FATHER DIVINE. WENT TO ETHIOPIA IN 1931 TO ORGANIZE EMPEROR

AS HE APPEARED IN 1953.

Geo LEE

GET THAT MAN OUT OF THE COUNTRY

WHEN THE BLACK EAGLE WRECKED THE EMPEROR'S PLANE HE WAS ORDERED OUT!

SELASSIE

SELASSIE'S ROYAL AIR-FORCE OF 3-PLANES. A CAPTAIN IN THE FINNISH AIR-FORCE IN 1940 AGAINST THE RUSSIANS. BECAME A COLONEL IN ENGLAND'S ROYAL AIR-FORCE. AFTER WORLD WAR II OPERATED AIR-FREIGHT IN LATIN AMERICA. ONE OF THE BEST KNOWN GUN RUNNERS. AMBASSADOR-AT-LARGE IN KATANGA IN EARLY '60's. RAN A SUGAR BROKERAGE FIRM IN N.Y. (1974)

1980 GEO L. LEE FEATURE SERVICE

FIRST BLACK

PRES. OF FRENCH SENATE

GASTON MONNERVILLE

CHAMPION OF RIGHTS FOR COLONIAL PEOPLES WAS ELECTED PRESIDENT OF THE COUNCIL OF THE FRENCH REPUBLIC IN 1947. THE FIRST BLACK COLONIAL... HE HELD THE OFFICE FOR OVER 20-YEARS. BORN IN CAYENNE, FRENCH GUIANA (1897) WHERE HE WAS EDUCATED. HE RECEIVED HIS LAW DEGREE FROM THE U. OF TOULOUSE IN FRANCE. A VERY SUCCESSFUL LAWYER HE ENTERED POLITICS IN 1932 AND SERVED IN THE FRENCH CHAMBER OF DEPUTIES FROM GUIANA AND UNDER SECRETARY OF STATE FOR COLONIES (1937-38). IN 1940 HE JOINED FRANCE'S UNDERGROUND MOVEMENT AGAINST THE NAZIS AND WAS DECORATED WITH THE MEDAILLE DE LA RESISTANCE. HE BECAME V-PRES., OF THE RADICAL SOCIALIST PARTY IN FRANCE. HE FOUNDED A TRADE SCHOOL FOR LEPER CHILDREN IN GUIANA THE – ECOLE MARCHAUK.

BLACK SLAVES FOUGHT FOR KING GEORGE IV DURING THE REVOLUTIONARY WAR. THEY WERE PROMISED FREEDOM BY THE BRITISH. AFTER THE WAR IN 1783, SHIPLOADS OF NEGROES WERE TAKEN TO NOVA SCOTIA. NEW YORK SLAVES TOOK ADVANTAGE OF THE BOATS TO ESCAPE FROM THEIR AMERICAN MASTERS.

A POLITICAL KINGMAKER

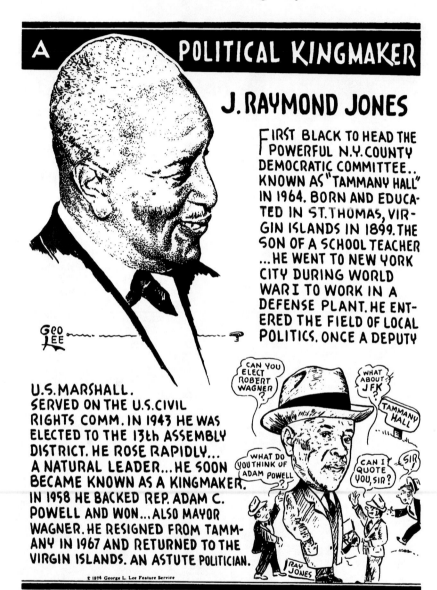

J. RAYMOND JONES

FIRST BLACK TO HEAD THE POWERFUL N.Y. COUNTY DEMOCRATIC COMMITTEE... KNOWN AS "TAMMANY HALL" IN 1964. BORN AND EDUCATED IN ST. THOMAS, VIRGIN ISLANDS IN 1899. THE SON OF A SCHOOL TEACHER ...HE WENT TO NEW YORK CITY DURING WORLD WAR I TO WORK IN A DEFENSE PLANT. HE ENTERED THE FIELD OF LOCAL POLITICS. ONCE A DEPUTY U.S. MARSHALL. SERVED ON THE U.S. CIVIL RIGHTS COMM. IN 1943 HE WAS ELECTED TO THE 13th ASSEMBLY DISTRICT. HE ROSE RAPIDLY... A NATURAL LEADER...HE SOON BECAME KNOWN AS A KINGMAKER. IN 1958 HE BACKED REP. ADAM C. POWELL AND WON...ALSO MAYOR WAGNER. HE RESIGNED FROM TAMMANY IN 1967 AND RETURNED TO THE VIRGIN ISLANDS. AN ASTUTE POLITICIAN.

THE LION of SWAZILAND

1899
1982

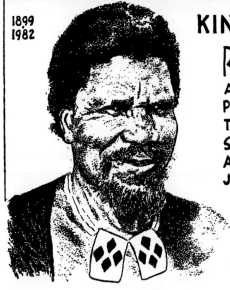

GEO
LEE

KING SOBHUZA II

REGARDED BY DIPLOMATS AS A POPULAR KING HELD IN AWE AND AFFECTION BY HIS PEOPLE. HE REIGNED OVER THE TINY MOUNTAIN KINGDOM OF SWAZILAND IN SOUTHEASTERN AFRICA FOR 60 YEARS. BORN ON JULY 22, 1899 AND WAS CROWNED KING ON DEC 22, 1921. HE HAD 100 WIVES AND IT WAS SAID HE FATHERED MORE THAN 500 CHILDREN. HIS KINGDOM A BRITISH PROTECTORATE, ACHIEVED INDEPENDENCE ON SEPT 6, 1968. AS KING HE HAD VOWED TO GIVE BACK LAND SEIZED BY WHITE SETTLERS IN THE 1890s. WHEN HE WAS CROWNED ONLY 37 PERCENT OF THE LAND WAS SWAZI. AT THE TIME OF HIS DEATH 73 PERCENT WAS BACK IN SWAZI HANDS. IN 1973 HE SUSPENDED THE BRITISH-INSPIRED CONSTITUTION TO RULE AS AN ABSOLUTE MONARCH. IN THE SWAZILAND TELEPHONE DIRECTORY HE WAS SIMPLY LISTED AS "HIS MAJESTY."

1982 GEO L. LEE FEATURE SERVICE

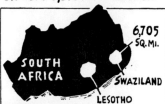

6,705 SQ. MI.

SOUTH AFRICA

SWAZILAND

LESOTHO

SWAZILAND (1968) POP. 600,000 INDUSTRY: SUGAR, CITRUS, RICE, COTTON, TOBACCO, PINEAPPLES. EXPORTS: IRON ORE, WOOD PULP, AND ONE OF THE WORLD'S LARGEST ASBESTOS MINES.

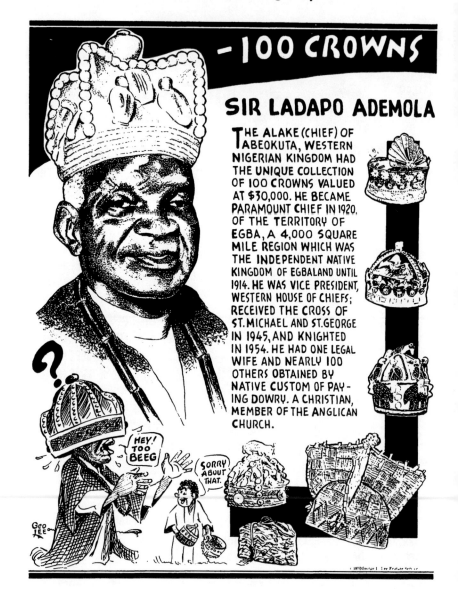

-100 CROWNS

SIR LADAPO ADEMOLA

THE ALAKE (CHIEF) OF ABEOKUTA, WESTERN NIGERIAN KINGDOM HAD THE UNIQUE COLLECTION OF 100 CROWNS VALUED AT $30,000. HE BECAME PARAMOUNT CHIEF IN 1920, OF THE TERRITORY OF EGBA, A 4,000 SQUARE MILE REGION WHICH WAS THE INDEPENDENT NATIVE KINGDOM OF EGBALAND UNTIL 1914. HE WAS VICE PRESIDENT, WESTERN HOUSE OF CHIEFS; RECEIVED THE CROSS OF ST. MICHAEL AND ST. GEORGE IN 1945, AND KNIGHTED IN 1954. HE HAD ONE LEGAL WIFE AND NEARLY 100 OTHERS OBTAINED BY NATIVE CUSTOM OF PAYING DOWRY. A CHRISTIAN, MEMBER OF THE ANGLICAN CHURCH.

60

60-YEARS of ENTERTAINING

MABEL MERCER

DIED 1984

Geo LEE

THE "GRANDE DAME" OF THE INTIMATE NIGHT CLUBS...WHO ONCE DREAMED OF BEING A MEZZO-SOPRANO. HER ELEGANCE OF STYLING AND LYRICS MADE HER THE TOAST OF N.Y. SUPPER CLUBS FOR MANY YEARS. BORN IN STAFFORDSHIRE, ENGLAND OF A BLACK FATHER AND A WHITE MOTHER. AT 14 SHE LEFT SCHOOL TO JOIN A SONG AND DANCE

GROUP THAT TOURED ENGLAND AND THE CONTINENT. IN 1924 SHE MET BRICKTOP THE CHICAGOAN SINGER-HOSTESS WHO HAD A NIGHT CLUB IN PARIS. BRICKTOP HELPED HER TO BECOME THE TOAST OF PARIS. SHE CAME TO N.Y.C. IN 1938 AND HAS BEEN A SHINING STAR EVER SINCE. IN 1972 AT 72 SHE WAS SINGING IN N.Y's ST. REGIS...

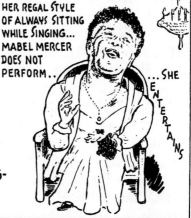

HER REGAL STYLE OF ALWAYS SITTING WHILE SINGING... MABEL MERCER DOES NOT PERFORM.. ...SHE ENTERTAINS

DR. RUFUS E. CLEMENT

1900
1967

OUTSTANDING EDUCATOR WAS THE FIRST NEGRO TO BE ELECTED (1953) AS A MEMBER OF A LARGE CITY BOARD OF EDUCATION IN THE DEEP SOUTH (ATLANTA) SINCE RECONSTRUCTION. DR. CLEMENT WHO WAS LISTED IN... "WHO'S WHO" FOR HIS ACHIEVEMENTS WAS BORN IN SALISBURY, N.C. HIS FATHER A BISHOP IN THE AME ZION CHURCH (LOUISVILLE, KY). DEAN OF LOUISVILLE MUNICIPAL COLLEGE (1931-37), BEFORE BECOMING PRESIDENT OF ATLANTA UNIVERSITY WHICH LASTED 30-YEARS. (1937-67)

ROBERT BROWN ELLIOTT

1842
1884

BRILLIANT LAWYER, ORATOR AND POLITICIAN WAS ELECTED TO THE U.S. CONGRESS AS A REPRESENT-ATIVE FROM SOUTH CAROLINA. HE SERVED IN THE 42nd AND 43rd (1871-74). BORN FREE IN BOSTON OF WEST INDIAN PARENTS. EDUCATED AT PRIVATE SCHOOLS IN BOSTON AND IN BRITISH W.I., AND HIGHBON ACADEMY IN LON-DON. GRADUATED FROM ENGLAND'S ETON COLLEGE WITH HONORS (1853). HE SERVED IN THE So. CAROLINA STATE LEGISLATURE IN 1868-70.

Geo LEE

1978 GEO L. LEE FEATURE SERVICE

62

ONE OF AMERICA'S TOP PAINTERS

HALE WOODRUFF

1900
2
1980

Known as the leading artist of the Harlem Renaissance and one of America's foremost art teachers. Born in Cairo, Ill., Mr. Woodruff was educated in the schools of Nashville. He began his study of painting at the Indianapolis Art Inst., then John Herron Art Inst...but lack of funds; was forced to drop-out. Luckily he won the Harmon Bronze Award and national recognition, funds became available. In 1926 went to Paris and studied at Moderne and the Scandinave Academies, and Henry O. Tanner. Returned to the U.S. in 1931 and accepted a teaching position at Atlanta U. Founded Atlanta's Art Dept. and taught 15-years. Established the first black artist annual exhibitions. Won many honors for his paintings. Professor of art at N.Y.U. in 1946. His innovative and mastery works earned him "Master Painter."

Geo Lee

As he appeared in 1946.

WHAT IS IT?

I DUNNO

ART EXHIBIT

r1980 GEO L. LEE FEATURE SERVICE

63

NOBEL PEACE PRIZE

ALBERT LUTHULI
1900-1967

FROM TEACHER IN A MISSIONARY COLLEGE IN SO. AFRICA TO ZULU CHIEF TO ELDER STATESMAN OF THE AFRICAN NAT'L CONGRESS. BORN IN SOUTHERN RHODESIA, HE WENT TO THE MISSION SCHOOLS IN THE UNIONS NATAL PROVINCE AND BECAME A TEACHER. IN 1935 HE LEFT TEACHING TO SERVE AS CHIEF OF HIS TRIBE. HE JOINED THE AFRICAN NAT'L CONGRESS IN 1945 AND ELECTED ITS LEADER IN 1952. LUTHULI WAS SPOKESMAN FOR SOUTH AFRICA'S MORE THAN 11-MILLION BLACKS. THE WHITE SO. AFRICAN GOV'T

Geo Lee

OSLO NORWAY

LUTHULI ACCEPTING NOBEL AWARD

CHARGED HIM WITH TREASON IN 1956...BUT WAS ACQUITTED. IN 1959 THEY BANISHED HIM TO HIS HOME DISTRICT. HE WAS AWARDED THE NOBEL PEACE PRIZE (1960) FOR HIS EFFORTS TO RID SO. AFRICA OF ITS WHITE SETTLER APARTHEID POLICY.

© 1975 George L. Lee Feature Service

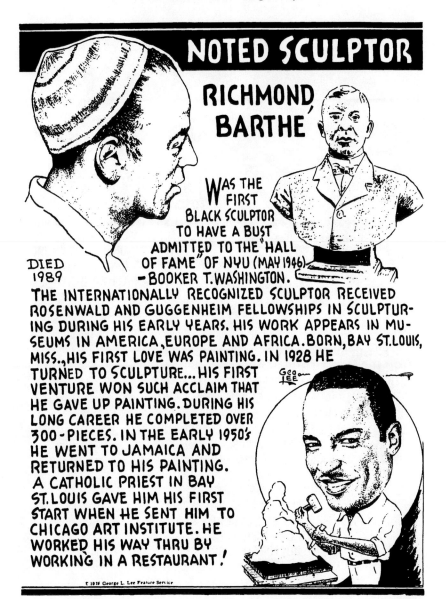

NOTED SCULPTOR

RICHMOND BARTHE

WAS THE FIRST BLACK SCULPTOR TO HAVE A BUST ADMITTED TO THE "HALL OF FAME" OF NYU (MAY 1946) — BOOKER T. WASHINGTON.

DIED 1989

THE INTERNATIONALLY RECOGNIZED SCULPTOR RECEIVED ROSENWALD AND GUGGENHEIM FELLOWSHIPS IN SCULPTUR-ING DURING HIS EARLY YEARS. HIS WORK APPEARS IN MU-SEUMS IN AMERICA, EUROPE AND AFRICA. BORN, BAY ST. LOUIS, MISS., HIS FIRST LOVE WAS PAINTING. IN 1928 HE TURNED TO SCULPTURE... HIS FIRST VENTURE WON SUCH ACCLAIM THAT HE GAVE UP PAINTING. DURING HIS LONG CAREER HE COMPLETED OVER 300-PIECES. IN THE EARLY 1950's HE WENT TO JAMAICA AND RETURNED TO HIS PAINTING. A CATHOLIC PRIEST IN BAY ST. LOUIS GAVE HIM HIS FIRST START WHEN HE SENT HIM TO CHICAGO ART INSTITUTE. HE WORKED HIS WAY THRU BY WORKING IN A RESTAURANT!

© 1978 George L. Lee Feature Service

65

- ONCE IN A HUNDRED YEARS.

MARIAN ANDERSON
DANBURY, CONN.

THE WORLD FAMOUS **CONTRALTO** WHOSE **VOICE** THE GREAT **ARTURO TOSCANINI** SAID," A VOICE LIKE YOURS IS HEARD ONCE IN A HUNDRED YEARS"– ONCE SANG FOR THE SUM OF $5.00 AT **CHURCH SOCIALS** AS A YOUNG GIRL IN PHILADELPHIA, HER BIRTHPLACE.

Geo Lee

HER **GREAT** CAREER WAS **LAUNCHED** BY THE **UNION BAPTIST CHURCH** WHO SENT HER TO **GIUSEPPE BOGHETTI,** FOREMOST VOICE TEACHER. IN 1925 SHE MADE HER DEBUT IN N.Y. CITY AT LEWISOHN STADIUM. ALTHO A SUCCESS, HER NEXT CONCERT WAS NOT. SHE WENT TO EUROPE AND SUCCESS. WHILE THERE, **SOL HUROK,** THE AMERICAN IMPRESARIO HEARD AND SIGNED HER IN 1935. IN 1955 SHE BECAME THE FIRST BLACK TO SING WITH THE METROPOLITAN OPERA CO. SHE WAS NAMED TO THE **U.S.** DELEGATION OF THE **U.N.** IN 1958. HER WORLD HONORS BY KINGS, NATIONS, CITIES AND UNIVERSITIES INCLUDED OVER 20 HONORARY DOCTORATE DEGREES – ALTHO SHE ONLY COMPLETED THE 12th GRADE.

SLAVE BOY TO HONOR CITIZEN!

BASHIR SHAMBE
OF TBILISI, GEORGIAN SOVIET RUSSIA

1. IN 1943 HE WAS A DELEGATE TO THE DISTRICT COMMITTEE OF THE COMMUNIST PARTY AT TBILISI. THE ONLY BLACK MAN AND HE WORE THE BADGE OF THE ORDER OF THE RED BANNER OF LABOR, AWARDED BY THE GEORGIAN SOVIET GOV'T. SUCH AN HONOR WAS BESTOWED ONLY ON THOSE WHO MERITED HIGH MARKS OF GRATITUDE OF THE PEOPLE BY EXCEPTIONAL ACHIEVEMENT AND DEVOTION: HIGHLY RESPECTED HE WAS A MEMBER OF THE GEORGIAN FIRE FIGHTING UNIT. SHAMBE WAS BORN IN TEHERAN, IRAN (PERSIA). HIS PARENTS CAME FROM AFRICA, THEY WERE SLAVES WHO HAD BEEN BOUGHT BY THE KHANS OF TEHERAN

2. FROM THE SLAVE MARKETS OF NORTH AFRICA. THE YOUNGEST OF FOUR CHILDREN. HIS FATHER DIED FROM OVERWORK. HIS MOTHER IN POOR HEALTH WAS PUT OUT INTO THE STREETS WITH HER CHILDREN AND "FREEDOM". HE WAS HIRED OUT TO A GEORGIAN PRINCE AND TAKEN TO GEORGIA. THEN THE REVOLUTION AND REAL FREEDOM. THE RUSSIANS TOOK OVER. SHAMBE JOINED THE RED ARMY - LIFE CHANGED - HE BECAME EDUCATED, LEARNED MACHINERY, ROSE RAPIDLY AS A CIVIC LEADER.

Geo Lee

1950 George L. Lee Feature Service

67

ALWAYS FOR PEACE

DR. RALPH J. BUNCHE
1904 - 1971

WHO BEGAN HIS CAREER AS AN EDUCATOR ONLY TO BECOME THE WORLD'S FIGHTER FOR **PEACE** AS A **U.N.** MEDIATOR. BORN IN DETROIT, ORPHANED AT AN EARLY AGE AND REARED BY HIS GRANDMOTHER. EDUCATED IN LOS ANGELES AND A GRADUATE OF **UCLA** WITH PHI BETA KAPPA HONORS. IN 1928, WITH A MASTERS FROM HARVARD **U.**, HE JOINED THE FACULTY OF HOWARD **U.**, IN POLITICAL SCIENCES. HE RETURNED TO HARVARD FOR HIS **PH.D** AND IN 1934 HE WON

THE **TOPPAN** PRIZE FOR HIS **ESSAY** ON SOCIAL SCIENCES. IN 1944 HE BECAME THE **FIRST** BLACK OFFICIAL IN THE **STATE** DEPT. IN 1946 HE TOOK A POST WITH THE **U.N.** AND DURING THE CRISIS IN PALESTINE ('48) HE TOOK OVER WHEN COUNT BERNADOTTE THE **U.N.** MEDIATOR WAS KILLED IN JERUSALEM. HIS EFFORTS BROUGHT FORTH PEACE. FOR THIS FEAT HE RECEIVED THE NOBEL PEACE PRIZE IN 1950 - THE FIRST BLACK. IN 1955 HE BECAME UNDER SECRETARY OF THE **U.N.** AND HELD THE POST UNTIL HE RETIRED IN 1971. A TROUBLESHOOTER FOR PEACE IN THE WORLD.

© 1972 George L. Lee Feature Service

LORD CONSTANTINE

BRITAIN'S FIRST BLACK *LORD!*

LEARIE CONSTANTINE A NATIVE OF TRINIDAD AND GRANDSON OF WEST INDIAN SLAVES. AN OUTSTANDING PROFESSIONAL CRICKET PLAYER WHO LED THE WEST INDIES OVER ENGLAND IN 1929. HE WAS THE FIRST BLACK RECTOR OF ST. ANDREWS UNIV., IN SCOTLAND. BECAME AMBASSADOR IN LONDON FOR TRINIDAD AND TOBAGO IN 1962-64. KNIGHTED A "SIR" IN 1962. A MEMBER OF THE SPORTS COUNCIL ON AMATEUR SPORTS IN 1965. A MEMBER OF BRITAIN'S RACE RELATIONS BOARD IN 1966. A GOVERNOR OF THE BBC IN 1968. QUEEN ELIZABETH APPOINTED HIM TO A LIFE PEERAGE IN 1969... THE FIRST BLACK LORD AT AGE 67. DIED 1971.

Geo Lee

FAMOUS GOSPEL SINGER

1925. 1973

IN 1956 —

♪ "SURELY GOD IS ABLE" ♪

CLARA WARD AND HER SINGING GROUP WHO ♪ ATTAINED INTERNATIONAL SUCCESS AT THE 1957 NEWPORT JAZZ FESTIVAL. CLARA STARTED SINGING IN CHURCH AT THE AGE OF 5. AS SHE GREW SHE JOINED HER MOTHER AND SISTER SINGING IN CHURCHES IN PHILA. AT 19 SHE TOOK OVER THE GROUP AND ON TO FAME AND FORTUNE. BY 1973 THEY HAD RECORDED 50-ALBUMS, CLARA HAD WRITTEN 500 SONGS!

© 1977 George L. Lee Feature Service

69

AFRICA'S IVORY COAST · LEADER

FÉLIX HOUPHOUET-BOIGNY

WHEN THE IVORY COAST WON ITS INDEPENDENCE IN 1960 FROM FRANCE... HE WAS ELECTED FIRST PRESIDENT. A NATIVE OF THE CAPITAL CITY - ABIDJAN... HE ONCE SERVED AS MAYOR. A WEALTHY PLANTATION OWNER AND A MEDICAL DOCTOR ..... A POWERFUL BLACK LEADER IN FRANCE'S POLITICS. HE BEGAN HIS CAREER IN 1946 WHEN HE WENT TO PARIS TO SERVE IN THE... FRENCH NATIONAL ASSEMBLY. IN 1956 HE BECAME THE FIRST AFRICAN MINISTER IN THE... FRENCH CABINET. IN 1959 HE

RETURNED TO THE IVORY COAST AS PRIME MINISTER...WON FREEDOM FROM FRANCE IN 1960. WHEN HE WAS A LAWMAKER HE ELIMINATED FORCED LABOR IN AFRICA. AT THE AGE OF 5 HE HELD THE RANK OF A TRIBAL CHIEF. HE WAS A SPOKESMAN FOR THE AFRICAN DEMOCRATIC RALLY THE POLITICAL PARTY OF BLACK AFRICA. AN OUTSTANDING LEADER!

3rd LARGEST EXPORTERS OF COFFEE IN THE WORLD!

COFFEE BEANS IVORY COAST

GOO LEE

70

DR. HASTINGS K. BANDA
PRIME MINISTER OF MALAWI

BORN IN 1906 OF PEASANT PARENTS IN NYASALAND, AFRICA. HIS FIRST LEARNING WAS IN THE LIVINGSTONIA MISSION. IN 1915 HE MADE A 1,000 MI. WALK TO SO. AFRICA FOR A BETTER EDUCATION. FOR 8 YEARS HE WORKED IN THE GOLDFIELDS AND STUDIED AT NIGHT. IN 1923 HE LEFT FOR THE U.S. HE STRUGGLED 15 YEARS FOR AN EDUCATION. BECAME A DOCTOR AT MEHARRY MEDICAL COLLEGE. WENT TO LONDON IN 1938 TO PRACTICE. HE RETURNED TO NYASALAND IN 1958 TO LEAD HIS PEOPLE. IT IS NOW - MALAWI - SINCE INDEPENDENCE IN '64

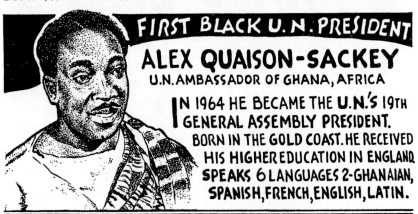

FIRST BLACK U.N. PRESIDENT
ALEX QUAISON-SACKEY
U.N. AMBASSADOR OF GHANA, AFRICA

IN 1964 HE BECAME THE U.N.'S 19TH GENERAL ASSEMBLY PRESIDENT. BORN IN THE GOLD COAST. HE RECEIVED HIS HIGHER EDUCATION IN ENGLAND. SPEAKS 6 LANGUAGES 2-GHANAIAN, SPANISH, FRENCH, ENGLISH, LATIN.

AUTHOR · LITERATURE PROF.

J. SAUNDERS REDDING

ONE OF AMERICA'S FINEST LITERARY ARTISTS AND EMERITUS PROFESSOR OF AMERICAN STUDIES AND HUMANE LETTERS, CORNELL UNIV.,(N.Y.). BORN IN WILMINGTON, DEL. ON OCT 13,1906. A PHI BETA KAPPA GRADUATE OF BROWN UNIV.,PH.D,M.A.,D.LITT. IN 1940 HE WAS INVITED BY THE U OF N.CAROLINA AND FUNDED BY THE ROSENWALD FOUNDATION. HE TRAVELED THRU THE SOUTH TO STUDY NEGRO LIFE. HE PUT HIS EXPERIENCES IN A BOOK-"NO DAY OF TRIUMPH"(1942) AND WON

"THE MAYFLOWER PRIZE" GIVEN ANNUALLY BY THE MAYFLOWER SOCIETY (N.C.) FOR BEST BOOK...THE FIRST BLACK. DR.REDDING GAINED NATIONAL ATTENTION.....A GUGGENHEIM SCHOLAR... HE TAUGHT AT SEVERAL BLACK COLLEGES AND PROFESSOR OF CREATIVE LITERATURE AT HAMPTON INSTI., FOR 24-YEARS. HIS LITERARY CONTRIBUTIONS WERE MANY!

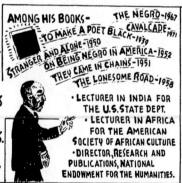

AMONG HIS BOOKS-
THE NEGRO-1967
TO MAKE A POET BLACK-1939
CAVALCADE-1971
STRANGER AND ALONE-1950
ON BEING NEGRO IN AMERICA-1952
THEY CAME IN CHAINS-1951
THE LONESOME ROAD-1958

- LECTURER IN INDIA FOR THE U.S. STATE DEPT.
- LECTURER IN AFRICA FOR THE AMERICAN SOCIETY OF AFRICAN CULTURE
- DIRECTOR, RESEARCH AND PUBLICATIONS, NATIONAL ENDOWMENT FOR THE HUMANITIES.

CONCERT ARTIST

AUBREY PANKEY
1906 - 1971

A NATIVE OF PITTSBURGH, PA., HE WAS ORPHANED AT THE AGE OF 15. HE WORKED AT ODD JOBS TO GET ENOUGH MONEY SAVED TO ENTER HAMPTON INSTITUTE AND STUDY ENGINEERING. BEFORE HE COULD GET SETTLED IN HIS STUDIES IT WAS DISCOVERED THAT HE HAD A SWEET BARITONE VOICE. AS A BOY SOPRANO HE HAD SUNG IN A PITTSBURGH BOYS' CHOIR. EN-COURAGED BY ROLAND HAYES THE DISTINGUISHED TENOR AND DR. R. NATHANIEL DETT, COMPOSER AND DIRECTOR OF MUSIC AT HAMPTON HE CHANGED TO MUSIC. HE RECEIVED SCHOLARSHIPS FROM OBERLIN CONSERVATORY OF MUSIC IN OHIO AND BOSTON U. IN 1930 HE SAILED TO EUROPE AND RETURNED AS A TOP-RANKING ARTIST IN 1940. HIS ARTISTRY BROUGHT ACCLAIM IN AMERICA. MR. PANKEY MADE HIS FIRST SOUTH AMERICA TOUR IN 1942. HE SANG IN CARNEGIE HALL IN 1944. HIS SECOND TOUR OF SOUTH AMERICA AND MEXICO WAS IN 1945. HE TRAVELED 15,000 MILES. HE WAS THE FIRST BLACK AMERICAN TO GIVE CONCERTS IN THAT PART OF THE WORLD. WHEN HE SANG IN SALZBURG IN 1933 THE NAZIS WERE COMING INTO POWER IN GERMANY AND HE WAS ONE OF THE VERY FIRST TO FEEL THEIR RACIAL HATRED, WHEN THEY DEMONSTRATED AGAINST HIM IN THE STREETS...BUT HIS CONCERT WAS A SUCCESS. HE WAS KILLED IN A CAR ACCIDENT IN EAST BERLIN, GERMANY IN 1971. HE LIVED THERE FOR 17-YEARS.

THE NOTED BARITONE GAVE CONCERTS IN THE WEST INDIES AND WAS THE FIRST AMERICAN TO MAKE A CONCERT TOUR OF PALESTINE.

73

AUTHOR · COMPOSER

1907
1977

Geo LEE

SHIRLEY GRAHAM DU BOIS

NOTED FOR HER BIOGRAPHIES OF FAMOUS BLACK PEOPLE, WRITTEN FOR THE YOUNG A NATIVE OF EVANSVILLE, IND., AND THE DAUGHTER OF A METHODIST MINISTER. IN 1929 HER FATHER BECAME HEAD OF A MISSION SCHOOL IN LIBERIA. SHIRLEY WENT ALONG BUT STOPPED IN PARIS TO STUDY MUSIC AT THE SORBONNE. IN 1930, RETURNED TO THE U.S. AND TAUGHT AT MORGAN STATE COLLEGE. SHE ENTERED OBERLIN COLLEGE AND RECEIVED HER B.A. AND MASTER'S DEGREES. IN 1951 SHE MARRIED DR. W.E.B. DU BOIS, THE BRILLIANT SCHOLAR. THEY LIVED IN GHANA FOR MANY YEARS AND BECAME CITIZENS. DURING WORLD WAR II SHE WAS A USO DIRECTOR IN ARIZ. ONCE COMPOSED A MUSICAL PLAY - "TOM-TOM" WHILE ATTENDING OBERLIN. HER MOST NOTED BIOGRAPHIES WERE ON - B.T. WASHINGTON, CARVER, ROBESON, BANNEKER AND DUBOIS.

MRS. DU BOIS' LAST WORK WAS A "PICTORIAL BIOGRAPHY OF W.E.B. DU BOIS."

•

DR. DU BOIS DIED IN GHANA AT THE AGE OF 95 (1963).

MRS. DU BOIS DIED IN PEKING, CHINA.

1979 GEO L. LEE FEATURE SERVICE

74

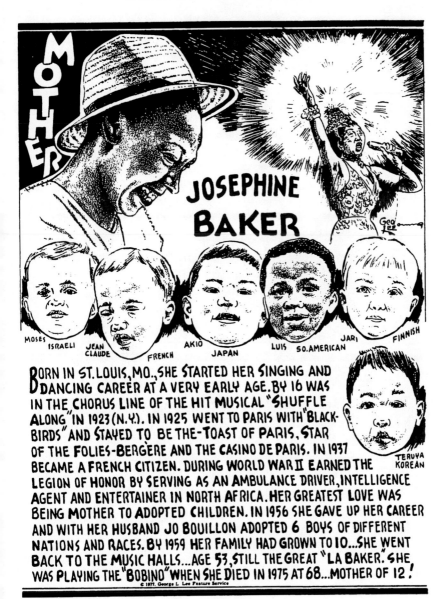

JOSEPHINE BAKER

MOSES ISRAELI • JEAN CLAUDE FRENCH • AKIO JAPAN • LUIS SO.AMERICAN • JARI FINNISH • TERUYA KOREAN

BORN IN ST. LOUIS, MO., SHE STARTED HER SINGING AND DANCING CAREER AT A VERY EARLY AGE. BY 16 WAS IN THE CHORUS LINE OF THE HIT MUSICAL "SHUFFLE ALONG" IN 1923 (N.Y.). IN 1925 WENT TO PARIS WITH "BLACK-BIRDS" AND STAYED TO BE THE-TOAST OF PARIS, STAR OF THE FOLIES-BERGERE AND THE CASINO DE PARIS. IN 1937 BECAME A FRENCH CITIZEN. DURING WORLD WAR II EARNED THE LEGION OF HONOR BY SERVING AS AN AMBULANCE DRIVER, INTELLIGENCE AGENT AND ENTERTAINER IN NORTH AFRICA. HER GREATEST LOVE WAS BEING MOTHER TO ADOPTED CHILDREN. IN 1956 SHE GAVE UP HER CAREER AND WITH HER HUSBAND JO BOUILLON ADOPTED 6 BOYS OF DIFFERENT NATIONS AND RACES. BY 1959 HER FAMILY HAD GROWN TO 10...SHE WENT BACK TO THE MUSIC HALLS...AGE 53, STILL THE GREAT "LA BAKER". SHE WAS PLAYING THE "BOBINO" WHEN SHE DIED IN 1975 AT 68...MOTHER OF 12!

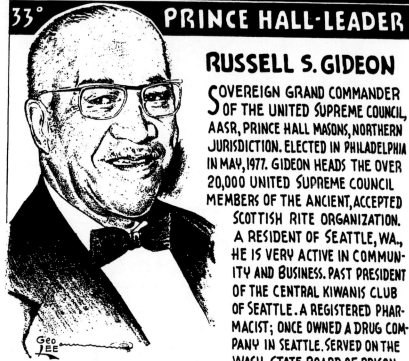

33° PRINCE HALL-LEADER

RUSSELL S. GIDEON

SOVEREIGN GRAND COMMANDER OF THE UNITED SUPREME COUNCIL, AASR, PRINCE HALL MASONS, NORTHERN JURISDICTION. ELECTED IN PHILADELPHIA IN MAY, 1977. GIDEON HEADS THE OVER 20,000 UNITED SUPREME COUNCIL MEMBERS OF THE ANCIENT, ACCEPTED SCOTTISH RITE ORGANIZATION. A RESIDENT OF SEATTLE, WA., HE IS VERY ACTIVE IN COMMUNITY AND BUSINESS. PAST PRESIDENT OF THE CENTRAL KIWANIS CLUB OF SEATTLE. A REGISTERED PHARMACIST; ONCE OWNED A DRUG COMPANY IN SEATTLE. SERVED ON THE WASH. STATE BOARD OF PRISON TERMS AND PAROLES. BORN IN LIVERPOOL, NOVA SCOTIA, CANADA. EARLY EDUCATION IN CALGARY WHERE HE WAS AN OUTSTANDING HIGH SCHOOL ATHLETE WHO WAS CREDITED WITH HAVING CAUGHT THE FIRST FORWARD PASS IN SENIOR FOOTBALL WHEN IT WAS MADE LEGAL IN CANADA (1928). HE RECEIVED HIS PHARMACY DEGREE IN BOSTON. HIS MANY ACTIVITIES ARE TREMENDOUS.

1978 GEO L. LEE FEATURE SERVICE

A LITTLE BIG... BUT IT'LL BE JUST FINE!

RUSS ROSE THRU THE RANKS OF THE SUPREME COUNCIL TO THE TOP-SOVEREIGN GRAND COMMANDER!

KEEP THE FAITH, BABY

ADAM CLAYTON POWELL
1908 – 1972

FLAMBOYANT AND CONTROVERSIAL CONGRESSMAN WHO EXILED TO BIMINI IN THE BAHAMAS (1966)

COOL BABY

BIMINI

Geo LEE

FIRST BLACK U.S. CONGRESSMAN ELECTED FROM THE EAST (N.Y.) IN 1944. BORN IN NEW HAVEN, CONN., AND REARED IN N.Y.C. HE RECEIVED HIS HIGHER EDUCATION FROM COLGATE (1930) AND COLUMBIA U. HE EARNED HIS DOCTOR OF DIVINITY FROM SHAW U., OF RALEIGH, N.C. ADAM FOLLOWED HIS FATHER AS PASTOR OF THE WORLD'S LARGEST BLACK BAPTIST CHURCH – THE ABYSSINIAN BAPTIST CHURCH IN HARLEM... AND HELD THE POST FOR 34-YEARS. FIRST BLACK ELECTED TO THE N.Y. CITY COUNCIL (1941). IN CONGRESS HE CHAMPIONED THE CAUSE OF THE LITTLE MAN. AS CHAIRMAN OF THE HOUSE, EDUCATION AND LABOR COMM., HE PASSED OVER 60-PIECES OF MEANINGFUL LEGISLATION. HE FOSTERED SUCH PROGRAMS AS – HEAD START, JOB CORPS, HIGHER MINIMUM WAGES, FEDERAL AID TO EDUCATION AND LOANS TO COLLEGE STUDENTS. A TREMENDOUS PIONEER IN CIVIL RIGHTS LONG BEFORE IT WAS POPULAR. A COLORFUL BAPTIST MINISTER, A POWERFUL POLITICIAN!

© 1974 George L. Lee Feature Service

IF HE HOLLERS LET HIM GO

1909
1984

CHESTER BOMAR HIMES

NOVELIST, AND ONE OF THE 20th CENTURY'S MOST PROLIFIC WRITERS, WROTE HIS FIRST NOVEL (1945),"IF HE HOLLERS LET HIM GO." IT BECAME A BEST SELLER AND WON A LITERARY AWARD. BORN IN JEFFERSON CITY, MO., SON OF SCHOOL TEACHERS. AT 17 HE ENROLLED AT OHIO STATE TO BE A DOCTOR. WHILE A BUS-BOY IN A CLEVELAND HOTEL HE HAD AN ACCIDENT...HE FELL DOWN AN ELEVATOR SHAFT. THE HOTEL GAVE HIM $5,-000 FOR HIS INJURIES. HE HAD TO DROP OUT OF SCHOOL. HE BEGAN TO DRIFT... UNTIL HE WAS ARRESTED FOR ARMED ROBBERY(1928). FACING INCARCERATION HE BOUGHT A TYPEWRITER. PAROLED IN 1936. HE MET RICHARD WRIGHT IN 1940 WHO ENCOURAGED HIM AS A WRITER AND TO MOVE TO PARIS. HE DID IN 1947. A PARIS PUBLISHER SUGGESTED DETECTIVE STORIES.

HIMES CREATED TWO DETECTIVE CHARACTERS-COFFIN ED SMITH AND GRAVEDIGGER JONES. HIS FIRST-"FOR THE LOVE OF IMABELLE," A BEST SELLER IN FRANCE...BEST DETECTIVE NOVEL OF THE YEAR! HE WROTE 8 MORE. HE WAS FAR MORE FAMOUS ABROAD THAN U.S. IN FRANCE WAS COMPARED TO DASHIELL HAMMETT. LEFT EUROPE IN 1965 MOVED TO SPAIN. DIED NOV 12,'84.

1985 GEO L. LEE FEATURE SERVICE

AMONG HIS MANY BOOKS!

COTTON COMES TO HARLEM
COME BACK CHARLESTON BLUE
THE LONELY CRUSADE 1947
A RAGE IN HARLEM 1965
PINK-TOES 1961
THIRD GENERATION 1954
QUALITY OF HURT 1972
BLACK ON BLACK 1973
MY LIFE OF ABSURDITY 1976

HE BEGAN WRITING SHORT STORIES IN PRISON. SOLD HIS FIRST STORY AFTER 5 YEARS TO ESQUIRE (1934). BECAME A LITERARY WRITER!

THE LAST KABAKA OF BUGANDA

SIR EDWARD W. F. MUTESA II

THE 36th KABAKA (KING), OF THE EAST AFRICAN KINGDOM OF BUGANDA THE LEADING PROVINCE OF UGANDA. A DESCENDANT OF A LINE THAT RULED BUGANDA FOR 900-YEARS. CROWNED KABAKA AT 17, HE SOON WENT TO LIVE IN LONDON. STUDIED AT CAMBRIDGE U., HONORARY CAPTAIN IN THE FAMED GRENADIER GUARDS. A "MAN ABOUT TOWN", HE WAS KNOWN AS KING FREDDIE. IN 1948 HE RETURNED TO HIS THRONE IN KAMPALA. LIGHTLY REGARDED BY HIS PEOPLE UNTIL HE DEMANDED INDEPENDENCE FOR BUGANDA.

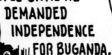

Geo LEE

KING FREDDIE DIED IN LONDON (1969)

BURIED IN ROYAL TOMB-KAMPALA (1971)

THE BRITISH REFUSED AND EXILED HIM TO LONDON (1953). AFTER 2-YEARS HE WAS RETURNED TO HIS JOYOUS PEOPLE... BUT THE BRITISH STRIPPED HIM OF HIS ABSOLUTE POWERS TO A CONSTITUTIONAL MONARCH. IN 1962 UGANDA WON INDEPENDENCE AND KING FREDDIE BECAME ITS FIRST PRESIDENT. IN 1966 PRIME MINISTER OBOTE OVERTHREW FREDDIE'S REIGN... JAILED HIS WIFE AND SON ... BUT HE ESCAPED AND FLED TO LONDON.

1980 GEO L. LEE FEATURE SERVICE

VIRGIN ISLES TO CAPITOL HILL

DR. MELVIN H. EVANS

FIRST BLACK REPUBLICAN ELECTED TO THE U.S. CONGRESS (1979) IN MORE THAN 40-YEARS...FROM THE VIRGIN ISLANDS. A NATIVE OF CHRISTIANSTED, ST. CROIX. A GRADUATE OF HOWARD UNIV., MEDICAL SCHOOL IN CARDIOLOGY. SERVED AS ASS'T HEALTH COMMISSIONER (1951-55), BECAME COMMISSIONER. IN 1961 WAS GIVEN A GRANT TO STUDY PUBLIC HEALTH AT THE U OF CALIF. ON HIS RETURN HE HAD BEEN REPLACED. HE WENT BACK INTO PRIVATE PRACTICE. A DEMOCRAT HE... CHANGED TO REPUBLICAN AND WAS APPOINTED GOVERNOR OF

THE VIRGIN ISLANDS BY PRES. NIXON IN 1969, THE FIRST BLACK NATIVE-BORN. IN 1971 THE FIRST ELECTED GOVERNOR. ELECTED FIRST BLACK CHAIRMAN OF THE SOUTHERN GOVERNOR'S CONFERENCE (1973). AS CONGRESSMAN HE WILL BE A "DELEGATE" AS THE VIRGIN ISLANDS HAS NO VOTE...LIKE DIST. OF COL.

1979 GEO L. LEE FEATURE SERVICE

THE BLACK CAUCUS IS VERY HAPPY TO HAVE DELEGATE EVANS AND HIS EXPERTISE ON CAPITOL HILL!

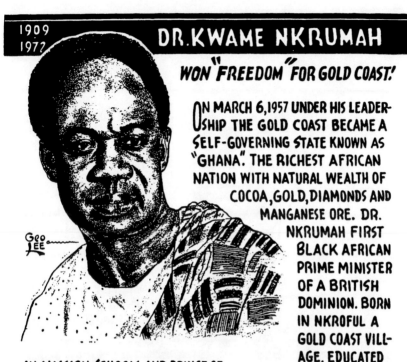

DR. KWAME NKRUMAH

1909
1972?

WON "FREEDOM" FOR GOLD COAST!

ON MARCH 6, 1957 UNDER HIS LEADER-SHIP THE GOLD COAST BECAME A SELF-GOVERNING STATE KNOWN AS "GHANA". THE RICHEST AFRICAN NATION WITH NATURAL WEALTH OF COCOA, GOLD, DIAMONDS AND MANGANESE ORE. DR. NKRUMAH FIRST BLACK AFRICAN PRIME MINISTER OF A BRITISH DOMINION. BORN IN NKROFUL A GOLD COAST VILL-AGE. EDUCATED IN MISSION SCHOOLS AND PRINCE OF WALES COLLEGE IN ACHIMOTA. 1935 TO THE U.S. AND LINCOLN U.(PA) A B.A. IN ECON-OMICS; LINCOLN THEOLOGICAL INSTITUTE (U OF PA) A THEOLOGY DEGREE. ON FACULTY AT LINCOLN U... PREACHED IN NY AND PA. TO ENGLAND (1945) FOR MORE STUDY BUT TURNED TO POLITICS. BECAME VERY ACTIVE IN WEST AFRICAN AFFAIRS. BACK HOME HE FORMED HIS CONVENTION PEOPLE'S PARTY (1949). THE PARTY WAS ELECTED IN 1951. HE WAS MADE PRIME MINISTER (1952) AND FOUGHT FOR FREEDOM!

NKRUMAH, THE FIRST PRESIDENT OF THE REPUBLIC OF GHANA. 1960

FREEDOM
FREEDOM

THE REDEEMER
THE MESSIAH

Geo Lee

© 1978 George L. Lee Feature Service

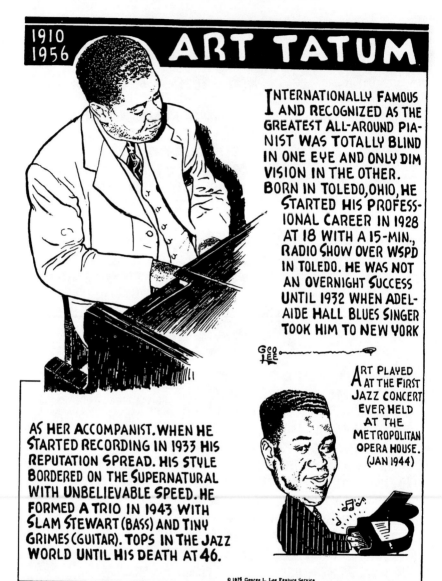

1910 1956 ART TATUM

INTERNATIONALLY FAMOUS AND RECOGNIZED AS THE GREATEST ALL-AROUND PIANIST WAS TOTALLY BLIND IN ONE EYE AND ONLY DIM VISION IN THE OTHER. BORN IN TOLEDO, OHIO, HE STARTED HIS PROFESSIONAL CAREER IN 1928 AT 18 WITH A 15-MIN., RADIO SHOW OVER WSPD IN TOLEDO. HE WAS NOT AN OVERNIGHT SUCCESS UNTIL 1932 WHEN ADELAIDE HALL BLUES SINGER TOOK HIM TO NEW YORK

Geo Lee

ART PLAYED AT THE FIRST JAZZ CONCERT EVER HELD AT THE METROPOLITAN OPERA HOUSE. (JAN 1944)

AS HER ACCOMPANIST. WHEN HE STARTED RECORDING IN 1933 HIS REPUTATION SPREAD. HIS STYLE BORDERED ON THE SUPERNATURAL WITH UNBELIEVABLE SPEED. HE FORMED A TRIO IN 1943 WITH SLAM STEWART (BASS) AND TINY GRIMES (GUITAR). TOPS IN THE JAZZ WORLD UNTIL HIS DEATH AT 46.

The IMPECCABLE·TEDDY WILSON

TRULY ONE OF THE GREAT JAZZ PIANISTS, A LEGEND IN HIS OWN TIME. BORN IN AUSTIN, TEXAS IN 1912. LIVED AND WENT TO SCHOOL AT TUSKEGEE INSTITUTE (ALA) WHERE HIS PARENTS WERE TEACHERS. QUALIFIED AS A LINOTYPE OPERATOR BUT THE COLOR-LINE STEPPED IN... SO HE TURNED TO HIS MUSIC. STARTED HIS CAREER IN DETROIT (1929) PLAYING WITH LOCAL BANDS. SOON TO CHICAGO AND ARMSTRONG, TATE AND NOONE. N.Y. CITY IN 1933 WITH BENNY CARTER TO RECORD WITH THE CHOCOLATE DANDIES. MADE NATIONAL NEWS IN 1935 WHEN HE JOINED BENNY GOODMAN

Geo Lee

A GREAT JAZZ STYLIST WHO HAS MADE AN IMPACT ON JAZZ PIANISTS EVERYWHERE...

AND GENE KRUPA MAKING A VERY BIG "TRIO." FORMED HIS OWN BAND IN 1939. RE-JOINED GOODMAN ON BROADWAY. (1945). A STAFF MUSICIAN ON WNEW AND CBS RADIO (NYC). TAUGHT PIANO IMPROVISATION AT JUILLIARD (1945-52). IN 1956, PLAYED HIMSELF IN THE MOVIE "THE BENNY GOODMAN STORY." WITH HIS OWN TRIO HE TRAVELS HERE AND ABROAD. IN 1978 STILL THE IMPECCABLE.

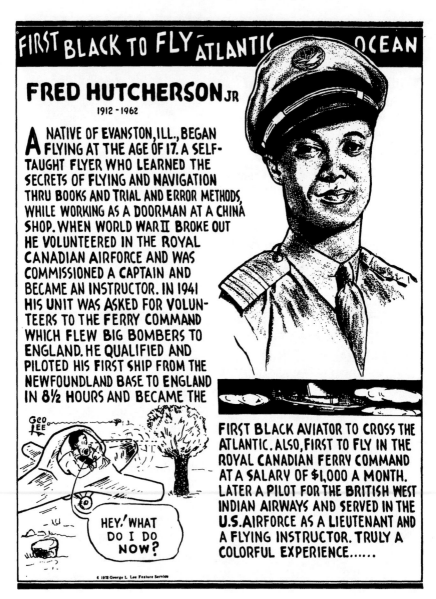

FIRST BLACK TO FLY ATLANTIC OCEAN

FRED HUTCHERSON JR
1912-1962

A NATIVE OF EVANSTON, ILL., BEGAN FLYING AT THE AGE OF 17. A SELF-TAUGHT FLYER WHO LEARNED THE SECRETS OF FLYING AND NAVIGATION THRU BOOKS AND TRIAL AND ERROR METHODS, WHILE WORKING AS A DOORMAN AT A CHINA SHOP. WHEN WORLD WAR II BROKE OUT HE VOLUNTEERED IN THE ROYAL CANADIAN AIRFORCE AND WAS COMMISSIONED A CAPTAIN AND BECAME AN INSTRUCTOR. IN 1941 HIS UNIT WAS ASKED FOR VOLUN-TEERS TO THE FERRY COMMAND WHICH FLEW BIG BOMBERS TO ENGLAND. HE QUALIFIED AND PILOTED HIS FIRST SHIP FROM THE NEWFOUNDLAND BASE TO ENGLAND IN 8½ HOURS AND BECAME THE

FIRST BLACK AVIATOR TO CROSS THE ATLANTIC. ALSO, FIRST TO FLY IN THE ROYAL CANADIAN FERRY COMMAND AT A SALARY OF $1,000 A MONTH. LATER A PILOT FOR THE BRITISH WEST INDIAN AIRWAYS AND SERVED IN THE U.S. AIRFORCE AS A LIEUTENANT AND A FLYING INSTRUCTOR. TRULY A COLORFUL EXPERIENCE......

NIGERIA'S FIRST PRIME MINISTER

SIR ABUBAKAR TAFAWA BALEWA

ON OCT 1,1960, NIGERIA THE WORLD'S LARGEST BLACK NATION WON ITS FREEDOM AND A "UNITED NIGERIA." IN 1957 SIR ABUBAKAR, A DEVOUT MOSLEM AND A FORMER SCHOOL TEACHER EMERGED AS THE FIRST PRIME MINISTER TO PREPARE FOR FREEDOM. BORN ABUBAKAR SON OF YAKUBU A MINOR OFFICIAL IN BAUCHI (No. NIGERIA). HIS NAME CAME FROM HIS VILLAGE-TAFAWA BALEWA, A REGION ALMOST ILLITERATE. HE RECEIVED SCHOOLING DUE TO HIS FATHER'S POSITION. HE WAS ALLOWED TO GO TO KATSINA TEACHERS' COLLEGE. HE TAUGHT AT A BOYS MIDDLE SCHOOL IN THE BAUCHI PLATEAU. A BORN TEACHER WITH A BRILLIANT MIND. NO NOR-

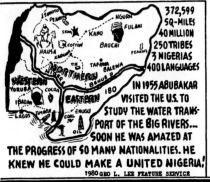

372,599 SQ-MILES
40 MILLION
250 TRIBES
3 NIGERIAS
400 LANGUAGES

IN 1955 ABUBAKAR VISITED THE U.S. TO STUDY THE WATER TRANSPORT OF THE BIG RIVERS... SOON HE WAS AMAZED AT THE PROGRESS OF SO MANY NATIONALITIES. HE KNEW HE COULD MAKE A UNITED NIGERIA.'

1980 GEO L. LEE FEATURE SERVICE

THERN NIGERIAN HAD PASSED THE EXAM FOR A SENIOR TEACHER'S CERTIFICATE. ABUBAKAR TOOK THE EXAM AND PASSED SO EASILY THAT LONDON UNIVERSITY'S INSTITUTE OF EDUCATION GRANTED HIM A SCHOLARSHIP IN 1945. A FINE ORATOR HE RETURNED HOME AND BECAME AN ADVOCATE FOR FREEDOM!

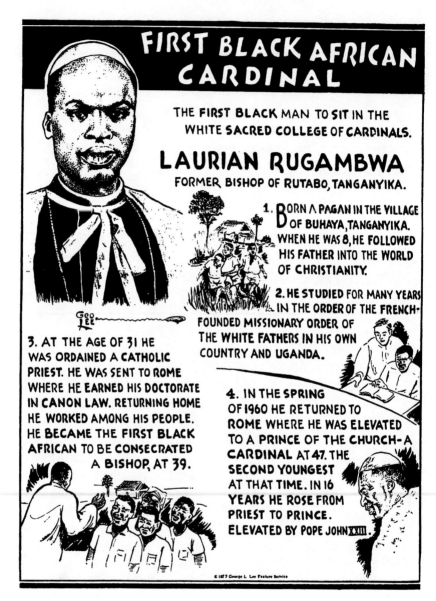

FIRST BLACK AFRICAN CARDINAL

THE FIRST BLACK MAN TO SIT IN THE WHITE SACRED COLLEGE OF CARDINALS.

LAURIAN RUGAMBWA

FORMER BISHOP OF RUTABO, TANGANYIKA.

1. BORN A PAGAN IN THE VILLAGE OF BUHAYA, TANGANYIKA. WHEN HE WAS 8, HE FOLLOWED HIS FATHER INTO THE WORLD OF CHRISTIANITY.

2. HE STUDIED FOR MANY YEARS IN THE ORDER OF THE FRENCH-FOUNDED MISSIONARY ORDER OF THE WHITE FATHERS IN HIS OWN COUNTRY AND UGANDA.

3. AT THE AGE OF 31 HE WAS ORDAINED A CATHOLIC PRIEST. HE WAS SENT TO ROME WHERE HE EARNED HIS DOCTORATE IN CANON LAW. RETURNING HOME HE WORKED AMONG HIS PEOPLE. HE BECAME THE FIRST BLACK AFRICAN TO BE CONSECRATED A BISHOP, AT 39.

4. IN THE SPRING OF 1960 HE RETURNED TO ROME WHERE HE WAS ELEVATED TO A PRINCE OF THE CHURCH—A CARDINAL AT 47. THE SECOND YOUNGEST AT THAT TIME. IN 16 YEARS HE ROSE FROM PRIEST TO PRINCE. ELEVATED BY POPE JOHN XXIII.

Geo Lee

© 1977 George L. Lee Feature Service

PSYCHOLOGIST

DR. KENNETH B. CLARK

NOTED EDUCATOR WHOSE KEEN UNDERSTANDING OF RACE RELATIONS IS OUTSTANDING. IN JULY 1975 HE RETIRED AS PROFESSOR OF PSYCHOLOGY AT THE CITY COLLEGE OF N.Y.C. AND PRESIDENT OF THE METROPOLITAN APPLIED RESEARCH CENTER INC., IN N.Y. A NATIVE OF PANAMA HE WAS RAISED IN N.Y. DR. CLARK HELPED TO FOUND THE

IN 1960 DR. CLARK WON NAACP'S 46th SPINGARN MEDAL-FOR "DISTINGUISHED MERIT AND ACHIEVEMENT."

46th SPINGARN MEDAL

WHITE SCHOOL

SEGREGATION

SOCIAL SCIENCE DOCUMENT

LINE OF

BLACK SCHOOL

Geo Lee

NORTHSIDE CENTER FOR CHILD DEVELOPMENT IN 1946. HE ALSO LAID THE GROUND FOR THE HARLEM YOUTH OPPORTUNITIES UNLIMITED A SELF-HELP YOUTH AGENCY WHICH CREATED FAR-REACHING REHABILITATION PROGRAMS IN HARLEM. HIS BEST KNOWN WORK- DARK GHETTO: DILEMMAS OF SOCIAL POWER.

HIS SOCIAL SCIENCE DOCUMENT CONTRIBUTED GREATLY TO THE HISTORIC SUPREME COURT SCHOOL DESEGREGATION. (1954)

1976 George L. Lee Feature Service

MISTER 'B'

BILLY **ECKSTINE**

VETERAN SHOWMAN WAS BORN IN PITTSBURGH IN 1914. HIS CAREER STARTED WHEN HE WON AN AMATEUR CONTEST IN WASH.,D.C. IN 1934. BY 1938 HE WAS SINGING AT THE CLUB DELISA IN CHICAGO. HIS RECORDING OF THE BLUES HIT "JELLY, JELLY" PUT HIM IN THE SPOTLIGHT. (1939) VERY TALENTED, HE DANCED, PLAYED A JAZZ TRUMPET AND MANY HORNS ALSO GUITAR... AND LED HIS BAND. AS A SINGLE HE TOURED EUROPE IN THE 1940's FOR 5-YEARS...PLAYING SUCH PLACES AS THE PALLADIUM IN LONDON AND PARIS. HIS BIG DEEP VOICE SINGING HIT SONGS AS, "I APOLOGIZE", "SOPHIS-TICATED LADY," MADE HIM A VERY BIG STAR. MR. B" STILL CONTINUED IN THE 1970's TO BE A BIG NIGHT CLUB ATTRACTION...

Geo LEE

MAN OF MANY FACES

Geo LEE

FRANK SILVERA
1914 - 1970

BRILLIANT CHARACTER ACTOR WHOSE CAREER STARTED IN BOSTON IN 1934. BORN IN JAMAICA OF A JEWISH FATHER AND A BLACK MOTHER. HE WAS RAISED IN BOSTON. ATTENDED BOSTON U., AND WHILE STUDYING LAW AT NORTHEASTERN LAW SCHOOL HE DECIDED TO SWITCH TO HIS FIRST LOVE OF ACTING. HIS EARLY EFFORTS WERE WITH THE BOSTON PLAYERS, NEW ENGLAND REPERTORY AND FEDERAL THEATRES. IN 1942 HE JOINED THE NAVY AND WHILE THERE HE WROTE, DIRECTED AND ANNOUNCED A RADIO SERIES FOR THE NAVY. HIS FIRST BROADWAY ROLE WAS "JOE" IN ANNA LUCASTA IN 1945. HIS STAR BEGAN TO RISE. AN EXPERT ON DIALECTS HIS VARIETY OF ROLES WAS TREMENDOUS. HIS ROLE OF "KING LEAR" IN SHAKESPEARE'S KING LEAR WAS PERHAPS HIS GREATEST. IN THE FILMS ONE OF HIS GREAT ROLES WAS IN "VIVA ZAPATA." HE APPEARED IN 100 FILMS AND TV. A REGULAR IN "HIGH CHAPPARAL" TV-SERIES, ROLES IN "THE NAME OF THE GAME," "RUN FOR YOUR LIFE" AMONG OTHERS.

IN KING LEAR

IN VIVA ZAPATA

IN VALDEZ IS COMING

HE ONLY PLAYED A BLACK MAN TWICE - IN A 36-YEAR CAREER!

© 1972 George L. Lee Feature Service

NOBEL PRIZE WINNER

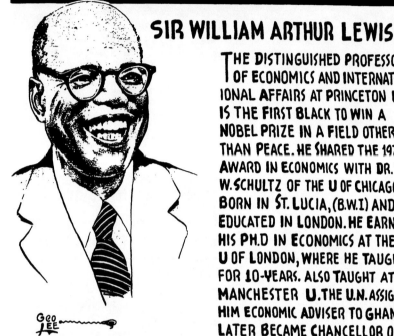

SIR WILLIAM ARTHUR LEWIS

THE DISTINGUISHED PROFESSOR OF ECONOMICS AND INTERNATIONAL AFFAIRS AT PRINCETON U., IS THE FIRST BLACK TO WIN A NOBEL PRIZE IN A FIELD OTHER THAN PEACE. HE SHARED THE 1979 AWARD IN ECONOMICS WITH DR. T. W. SCHULTZ OF THE U OF CHICAGO. BORN IN ST. LUCIA, (B.W.I) AND EDUCATED IN LONDON. HE EARNED HIS PH.D IN ECONOMICS AT THE U OF LONDON, WHERE HE TAUGHT FOR 10-YEARS. ALSO TAUGHT AT MANCHESTER U. THE U.N. ASSIGNED HIM ECONOMIC ADVISER TO GHANA. LATER BECAME CHANCELLOR OF GHANA U. IN 1963 WAS KNIGHTED BY QUEEN ELIZABETH II FOR HIS SERVICES AS VICE-CHANCELLOR OF THE UNIV. OF THE WEST INDIES. LEWIS JOINED PRINCETON IN 1963. THE 65-YEAR OLD PROFESSOR HAS A DEEP CONCERN FOR THE DEVELOPMENT OF THE THIRD WORLD NATIONS. AUTHOR OF 12-BOOKS. A BRILLIANT MAN!

Geo LEE

1980 GEO L. LEE FEATURE SERVICE

NOBEL PRIZE IN ECONOMICS
- SIR W. ARTHUR LEWIS
- THEODORE W. SCHULTZ

BOTH WINNERS SHARED $193,000.00—

1979

THEY WERE HONORED BECAUSE...THEY ARE-"DEEPLY CONCERNED ABOUT NEED AND POVERTY IN THE WORLD AND ARE ENGAGED IN FINDING WAYS OUT OF UNDER-DEVELOPMENT....THE SWEDISH ACADEMY.

WORLD FAMED SCHOLAR

DR. JOHN HOPE FRANKLIN

THE DISTINGUISHED PROFESSOR OF THE HISTORY DEPARTMENT AT THE UNIV. OF CHICAGO, WAS BORN IN RENTIESVILLE OKLA. HIS FATHER WAS A LAWYER AND POSTMASTER. AT THE AGE OF 10 THE FAMILY MOVED TO TULSA. HE WORKED HIS WAY THRU FISK UNIV., BY WAITING ON TABLES, GRADUATING IN 1935. HE RECEIVED HIS M.A. AND PH.D DEGREES AT HARVARD. HIS TEACHING CAREER BEGAN AT HOWARD UNIV. HE HELPED PREPARE THE NAACP'S BRIEF AGAINST SCHOOL SEGREGATION IN THE U.S. IN 1954. BECAME FIRST

Geo. Lee

BLACK DEPT. HEAD AT BROOKLYN COLLEGE IN 1956. HE WENT TO ENGLAND IN 1963 TO SERVE AS A VISITING PITT. PROF. OF AMERICAN HISTORY AT CAMBRIDGE UNIV. IN 1964 HE JOINED THE U OF CHICAGO FACULTY. A BRILLIANT LECTURER HE HAS APPEARED ALL OVER THE WORLD. AN AUTHOR OF 7 BOOKS. A MEMBER OF THE FULBRIGHT BOARD THAT SELECTS THE FULBRIGHT SCHOLARS. ONE OF THE MOST NOTABLE AUTHORITIES ON THE BLACK MAN'S PAST IN AMERICA.

WHY DID NAT TURNER REVOLT?

WELL YOU SEE HE WANTED TO....ER THESE ORCHIDS ARE BEAUTIFUL.

HIS HOBBY IS GROWING ORCHIDS IN HIS GREENHOUSE ON THE THIRD FLOOR OF HIS HOME.

270 POUNDS OF JOY

JUNE RICHMOND
1915 – 1962

A TOP JAZZ AND BLUES SINGER WHO BECAME A COMEDIENNE STAR IN SWEDEN. SHE STARTED HER SINGING CAREER AT CHICAGO'S VENDOME THEATER AT THE AGE OF 13, SINGING "AH, SWEET MYSTERY OF LIFE". AT 15 SHE WAS DANCING IN THE CHORUS LINES OF NIGHT CLUBS. SHE MOVED UP TO A BAND VOCALIST WITH CAB CALLOWAY, FLOYD RAY AND THE GREAT ANDY KIRK. HER RECORDINGS BECAME HITS. FAMED BAND LEADER JIMMY DORSEY DISCOVERED HER IN A SAN DIEGO CAFE.

I HOPE I'M GAINING

PLEASE, LADY HAVE A HEART!

AMBITION – TO SING OPERA!

THE REALLY BIG BREAK CAME WHEN SHE SANG A POLITICAL SONG ON THE RADIO DURING THE 1944 ROOSEVELT PRESIDENTIAL CAMPAIGN. BROADWAY PRODUCERS SIGNED HER FOR "ARE YOU WITH IT" A MUSICAL COMEDY WHICH TOOK HER TO EUROPE AND SUCCESS. SHE CHANGED TO A COMEDIENNE AND WAS A SENSATION IN SWEDEN AND THE EUROPEAN CLUBS. JUNE GAVE UP HER U.S. CITIZENSHIP TO REMAIN IN SWEDEN. 270 POUNDS OF JOY – DIED IN GÖTEBORG IN 1962.

GEO. LEE

© 1972 George L. Lee Feature Service

COMBAT GENERAL ★★

MAJ. GENERAL
FREDERIC E. DAVISON

THE THIRD BLACK IN **U.S.** MILITARY HISTORY TO WIN A GENERAL'S STAR AND THE FIRST IN A BATTLE COMMAND. HE ATTENDED THE PUBLIC SCHOOLS IN WASH, D.C. RECEIVED A MASTERS DEGREE IN ZOOLOGY FROM HOWARD U. IN 1940. A 2nd LT., IN THE INFANTRY RESERVES (1939). SERVED IN WORLD WAR II. LATER ACCEPTED A REGULAR ARMY COMMI-

Geo LEE

SSION. FIRST BLACK TO ENTER THE ARMY WAR COLLEGE. PROMOTED TO MAJ. GEN. (1971). FIRST BLACK TO COMMAND A DIVISION IN 1972...THE 8th INFANTRY IN WEST GERMANY. TOOK COMMAND OF THE MILITARY DISTRICT OF WASH, D.C. (1973). AFTER 35-YEARS OF OUTSTANDING ARMY SERVICE HE RETIRED IN 1974. *"A BRILLIANT CAREER"*

THE 199th LIGHT INFANTRY BRIGADE, BINH CHANH, SO. VIETNAM.

GEN. CREIGHTON ABRAMS, U.S. MILITARY COMMANDER IN VIETNAM, PINS THE SILVER STAR OF BRIG. GENERAL ON COL. DAVISON, ON THE FIELD OF COMBAT-1968.

© 1978 George L. Lee Feature Service

93

FIRST LADY LORD MAYOR

MRS. IRIS KING

THE FIRST WOMAN MAYOR OF KINGSTON, JAMAICA AND ITS 40TH MAYOR AND THE FIRST LADY MUNICIPAL HEAD IN BRITISH WEST INDIES 3-CENTURY HISTORY ... IN APRIL 1958. CITY COUNCILORS ELECTED BY THE VOTERS, IN TURN ELECT THE MAYOR. A DEADLOCK BETWEEN MRS. KING AND A LABOR PARTY MEMBER... A COIN WAS FLIPPED AND SHE WON. IN 1958 THE POPULATION WAS 350,000 AND THE 6TH LARGEST HARBOR IN THE WORLD. MRS. KING, MOTHER OF 5, HAD 19 YEARS OF POLITICAL EXPERIENCE WITH 3-YEARS OF POLITICAL TRAINING AT CHICAGO'S ROOSEVELT UNIV., AND AS A CITY COUNCILOR.

GEO LEE

BRIDGE BUILDER

ARCHIE A. ALEXANDER
OF DES MOINES, IOWA

ONE OF THE MOST OUTSTANDING BLACK STRUCTURAL ENGINEERS IN THE MID-WEST DURING THE 1930'S AND 40'S. A GRADUATE OF THE IOWA SCHOOL OF ENGINEERING. HE BUILT BRIDGES; A 37-MILE SEWAGE DISPOSAL SYSTEM IN SOUTH DES MOINES; THE JAMES RIVER VIADUCT AT MITCHELL, So. DAK; AIRPORTS; POWER PLANTS AND THE MULTI MILLION DOLLAR FREEWAY IN WASH, D.C.

© 1973 George L. Lee Feature Service

94

POSSESSOR OF A VOICE OF RAREST *BEAUTY*

DOROTHY MAYNOR

OF NEW YORK CITY

WAS BORN IN NORFOLK, VA., THE DAUGHTER OF A METHODIST MINISTER. HER FIRST SINGING WAS WITH THE CHILDREN'S CHOIR IN THE SUNDAY SCHOOL. SHE RECEIVED HER EDUCATION AT HAMPTON INSTITUTE. ALTHO SHE ENTERED THE COLLEGE IN HOME ECONOMICS SHE MAJORED IN MUSIC. AS A MEMBER OF THE HAMPTON CHOIR SHE GAINED A FINE BACKGROUND. HER BIG BREAK CAME IN 1939 WHEN SHE AUDITIONED FOR THE CELEBRATED CONDUCTOR, SERGE KOUSSEVITZKY. FROM THEN ON HER CAREER AS A SOPRANO ROSE TO THE HEIGHTS AS A CONCERT ARTIST. IN 1963 SHE FOUNDED THE – SCHOOL OF THE ARTS IN HARLEM. A CULTURAL CENTER LOCATED AT ST. JAMES PRESBY., CHURCH PASTORED BY REV. ROOKS, HER HUSBAND. AS DIRECTOR SHE IS THE GUIDING LIGHT OF BLACK YOUTH.

ONLY 4'8" SHE STANDS 6 FEET TALL IN HER EFFORTS.

Geo LEE

© 1972 George L. Lee Feature Service

95

FIRST NAVY HERO OF WORLD WAR II

DORIE MILLER
1919 - 1943

MESS ATTENDANT ABOARD THE S.S. ARIZONA, A BATTLESHIP OF THE U.S. NAVY. WHO BY HIS GLOWING DEEDS BECAME A HERO ON DEC 7, 1941 THE DAY OF THE INFAMOUS SNEAK ATTACK ON PEARL HARBOR BY THE JAPANESE... DORIE MANNED A MACHINE GUN WHEN MEMBERS OF THE CREW HAD BEEN PUT OUT OF ACTION.. AND SHOT DOWN 4 JAP PLANES... AFTER HE HAD CARRIED HIS WOUNDED CAPTAIN TO SAFETY... DORIE HAD NEVER MANNED A MACHINE GUN BEFORE THAT DAY! SON OF A SHARECROPPER HE WAS BORN NEAR WACO, TEXAS. HE LOST HIS LIFE WHILE HE WAS SERVING ON THE AIRCRAFT CARRIER LISCOMBE BAY... IT WAS SUNK ON NOV 24, 1943.

FOR HIS GALLANT DEEDS UNDER FIRE HE RECEIVED THE NAVY CROSS ON MAY 27, 1942.

DOMINICA'S - PRIME MINISTER

MARY EUGENIA CHARLES

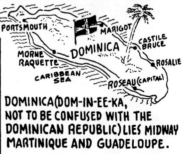

FIRST WOMAN PRIME MINISTER IN THE ENGLISH-SPEAKING CARIBBEAN. ELECTED ON JULY 21, 1980 TO GOVERN THE LITTLE ISLAND OF DOMINICA, POP: 80,000. IN 1979 TWO HURRICANES HAD NEARLY DESTROYED ITS ECONOMY. UNDER HER LEADERSHIP RECOVERY IS PROGRESSING. SHE RECEIVED HER EARLY SCHOOLING IN HER NATIVE DOMINICA. STUDIED LAW IN TORONTO AND LONDON. RETURNED IN 1949 TO PRACTICE LAW. ENTERED POLITICS...FOUGHT CORRUPTION IN GOVERNMENT. ORGANIZED THE DOMINICA FREEDOM PARTY (1968). FAILED TO WIN A SEAT IN 1970.

Geo LEE

WON IN 1975 AND HEADED THE OPPOSITION. AIDED IN THE INDEPENDENCE FROM BRITAIN, GRANTED IN 1978...HELPED TO OUST PRIME MINISTER PATRICK JOHN'S CORRUPTION. HER PARTY WON 17 OF 21 SEATS FOR A 5-YEAR TERM. AT 62, THE ONLY BLACK WOMAN TO HEAD A NATION!

DOMINICA (DOM-IN-EE-KA, NOT TO BE CONFUSED WITH THE DOMINICAN REPUBLIC) LIES MIDWAY MARTINIQUE AND GUADELOUPE.

1981 GEO L. LEE FEATURE SERVICE

BARITONE

WILLIAM WARFIELD

INTERNATIONALLY RENOWNED CONCERT SINGER WAS BORN IN WEST HELENA, ARK. SON OF A BAPTIST MINISTER. THE FAMILY MOVED TO ROCHESTER, N.Y., WHERE HE WENT TO SCHOOL. SINGING CAREER STARTED AS A BOY SOPRANO IN HIS FATHER'S CHURCH. AT 18, WON SINGING CONTEST AT THE NAT'L MUSIC EDUCATORS CONVENTION IN ST. LOUIS AND A SCHOLARSHIP. HE STUDIED AT EASTMAN SCHOOL OF MUSIC (ROCHESTER). WORKING ON HIS MASTER'S, THE ARMY CALLED HIM. WHILE IN THE SERVICE HE AUDITIONED FOR A PART IN THE MUSICAL "CALL ME MISTER"... AND MADE IT. HIS RECITAL DEBUT IN NY'S TOWN HALL (1950)..."SHOWBOAT" (1951), "PORGY AND BESS" (1952). HIS RICH BARITONE VOICE FOUND ITS WAY TO THE CONCERT STAGES OF THE WORLD. LIKE OL'MAN RIVER, HE STILL KEEPS ROLLIN' ALONG!

OL' MAN RIVER

AS JOE IN "SHOWBOAT," HIS RENDITION OF "OL'MAN RIVER" WILL NEVER BE FORGOTTEN...... WARFIELD ENDS EVERY CONCERT WITH THIS TREMENDOUS SONG

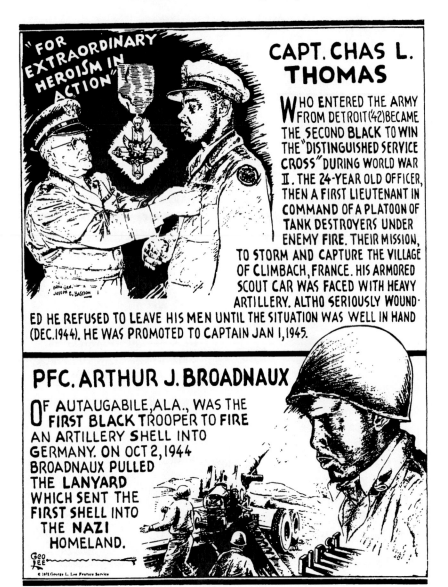

"FOR EXTRAORDINARY HEROISM IN ACTION"

CAPT. CHAS L. THOMAS

WHO ENTERED THE ARMY FROM DETROIT (42) BECAME THE SECOND BLACK TO WIN THE "DISTINGUISHED SERVICE CROSS" DURING WORLD WAR II. THE 24-YEAR OLD OFFICER, THEN A FIRST LIEUTENANT IN COMMAND OF A PLATOON OF TANK DESTROYERS UNDER ENEMY FIRE. THEIR MISSION, TO STORM AND CAPTURE THE VILLAGE OF CLIMBACH, FRANCE. HIS ARMORED SCOUT CAR WAS FACED WITH HEAVY ARTILLERY. ALTHO SERIOUSLY WOUNDED HE REFUSED TO LEAVE HIS MEN UNTIL THE SITUATION WAS WELL IN HAND (DEC.1944). HE WAS PROMOTED TO CAPTAIN JAN 1, 1945.

PFC. ARTHUR J. BROADNAUX

OF AUTAUGABILE, ALA., WAS THE FIRST BLACK TROOPER TO FIRE AN ARTILLERY SHELL INTO GERMANY. ON OCT 2, 1944 BROADNAUX PULLED THE LANYARD WHICH SENT THE FIRST SHELL INTO THE NAZI HOMELAND.

Geo LEE

© 1972 George L. Lee Feature Service

NATIONAL BAPTIST LEADER

DR. JOSEPH H. JACKSON

THE RELIGIOUS LEADER AND PRESIDENT OF THE 6.5 MILLION-MEMBER NATIONAL BAPTIST CONVENTION. HE HAS BEEN PASTOR OF THE OLIVET BAPTIST CHURCH IN CHICAGO SINCE 1941. AN ALUMNUS OF JACKSON COLLEGE (MISS). HE SERVED AS A MEMBER OF THE CENTRAL COMMITTEE OF THE WORLD COUNCIL OF CHURCHES AND WAS A DELEGATE TO THE FIRST SESSION OF THE COUNCIL IN AMSTERDAM, HOLLAND. A WORLD-TRAVELER TO AFRICA, ASIA, EUROPE AND THE MIDDLE

SERVED 1953-82

Geo Lee

EAST ON PREACHING MISSIONS. HE WAS INVITED TO THE 1962 SECOND VATICAN COUNCIL IN ROME BY POPE JOHN XXIII. A PROLIFIC-WRITER... AUTHOR OF MANY BOOKS-" MANY, BUT ONE," "UNHOLY SHADOWS," "FREEDOMS HOLY LIGHT"... AMONG THEM.'

DR. JACKSON CARRIED THE MESSAGE OF CHRISTIANITY BEHIND THE IRON CURTAIN AND CONDUCTED A PREACHING MISSION IN RUSSIA IN 1955.

1979 GEO L. LEE FEATURE SERVICE

MAURICE CARDINAL OTUNGA

GEO
LEE

ONE OF FIVE BLACK CARDINALS IN THE CATHOLIC CHURCH IN AFRICA. BORN THE SON OF A CHIEF OF THE BUKUSA TRIBE IN THE WESTERN PART OF KENYA. HE STUDIED CHRISTIANITY IN THE MISSION SCHOOLS. AT THE AGE OF 12, WAS RECEIVED IN THE CATHOLIC CHURCH. ENTERED A SEMINARY AT 21 AND WAS ORDAINED A PRIEST IN ROME AT 27. ONE YEAR AT THE VATICAN THEN RETURNED TO KENYA TO TEACH. IN 1957 HE WAS THE FIRST KENYA-BORN TO BECOME A BISHOP. IN 1971... ELEVATED TO ARCHBISHOP OF NAIROBI. TWO YEARS LATER (1973) HE WAS NAMED CARDINAL AT THE AGE OF 51 AND BECAME THE SPIRITUAL LEADER OF A "PARISH" OF NEARLY 12-MILLION TRIBESPEOPLE. OTHER AFRICAN COUNTRIES WITH BLACK CARDINALS ARE ZAIRE, UPPER VOLTA, MADAGASCAR AND TANZANIA (1975). THREE AFRICAN POPES IN HISTORY: ST. VICTOR (189-199), ST. MELCHIADES (311-312), AND ST. GELASIUS (492-496).

1978 Geo L. Lee Feature Serv

TOP PUBLISHER

JOHN H. JOHNSON

OUTSTANDING BLACK PUBLISHER IN AMERICAN HISTORY. RISING FROM A CHICAGO "KITCHEN OFFICE" WHERE HE EDITED AN IDEA AND WITH $500 PUBLISHED HIS FIRST MAGAZINE -THE NEGRO DIGEST...IN 1942. BORN IN ARKANSAS CITY, ARK., POP. 783. HE ATTENDED HIGH SCHOOL IN CHICAGO ALSO U. OF CHICAGO AND NORTHWESTERN U. WHILE WORKING IN THE OFFICE OF THE SUPREME LIBERTY LIFE INS. CO., HE EDITED THE COMPANY PAPER. IT'S POPULARITY GAVE HIM THE "IDEA" OF A BLACK MAGAZINE. IN 1945 HE LAUNCHED "EBONY"...

Geo LEE

PATTERNED AFTER "LIFE" MAGAZINE, "EBONY" ZOOMED INTO OUTER SPACE OF SUCCESS. THEN "JET" A SMALL NEWS DIGEST AND "BLACK WORLD", "BLACK STARS" AND "EBONY JR". THEY BUILT AN EMPIRE OF SUCCESS ...AN 8-MILLION DOLLAR OFFICE BUILDING...RADIO STATION... COSMETICS. HIS ACHIEVEMENT-BLACK PRIDE!

© 1977. George L. Lee Feature Service

"JOHN H. JOHNSON DAY" HARVARD UNIV - 1975

HONORARY DOCTOR OF HUMANE LETTERS SYRACUSE U - 1972 NORTHWESTERN U - 1974

PRESIDENTIAL AWARD FOR EXCELLENCE - U OF CINCIN. 1976

JPC

"PUBLISHER OF THE YEAR" 1972 - MAGAZINE PUBLISHERS ASS'N.

NAACP's SPINGARN MEDAL OF DISTINGUISHED ACHIEVEMENT 1966

ALL-TIME BLACK PUBLISHER BLACK PRESS 1977

MAN OF THE YEAR - 1973 PRINCE HALL MASONS

EBONY

SAMUEL L. GRAVELY JR.

FROM ENSIGN TO REAR ADMIRAL! THE FIRST BLACK TO GRADUATE FROM THE NAVY MIDSHIPMAN'S SCHOOL AT COLUMBIA U. THE FIRST TO BE ASSIGNED TO A NAVY COMBAT SHIP... AS COMMUNICATIONS OFFICER IN 1944. BECAME A

ENSIGN

Geo Lee

RADIO OFFICER ON THE BATTLESHIP IOWA AS A LIEUTENANT IN 1952. IN 1961 WAS THE FIRST BLACK TO COMMAND A NAVAL VESSEL AS... LT.COM. IN 1962 BECAME CAPTAIN OF THE USS FALGOUT, A COMBAT DESTROYER ESCORT RADAR CRAFT. IN 1966 TOOK OVER THE BIG USS. TAUSSIG.. A $20-MILLION SHIP!

CAPTAIN

ON JUNE 2, 1971 HE WAS ASSIGNED TO THE USS. JOUETT, A GUIDED MISSILE FRIGATE... AS THE FIRST BLACK ADMIRAL! ...REAR ADMIRAL IN 1972 AND DIRECTOR OF NAVAL COMMUNICATIONS. BORN IN RICHMOND, VA (1922)... HE WAS ONCE-A RAILWAY POSTAL CLERK.

ADMIRAL

© 1975 George L. Lee Feature Service

103

TANZANIA

JULIUS K. NYERERE

PRESIDENT OF THE UNITED RE-PUBLIC OF TANZANIA (ONCE TANGANYIKA AND ZANZIBAR). THE LEADER OF OVER 15-MILLION PEOPLE COVERING 364,500 SQ MILES. BORN IN 1922 THE SON OF THE CHIEF OF THE ZANAKI TRIBE IN THE VILLAGE OF BUTIAMA NEAR LAKE VICTORIA. HE ATTENDED MISSION SCHOOLS NEAR HIS HOME AND AT MAKERERE UNIV., IN UGANDA, AND STUDIED PHILOSOPHY, POLITICAL ECONOMY AND SOCIAL ANTHROPOLOGY AT EDINBURGH UNIV., IN SCOTLAND. HE BECAME A SCHOOL TEACHER. IN 1954, ELECTED HEAD OF THE TANGANYIKA AFRICAN NAT'L UNION AND WORKED ZEALOUSLY ALL HIS LIFE FOR LIBERATION. MR. NYERERE LED HIS NATION TO INDEPENDENCE FROM GRT. BRITAIN IN 1961 AND BECAME PRIME MINISTER. IN 1962 WAS ELECTED THE FIRST PRESIDENT.

ELECTED PRESIDENT OF THE SIXTH PAN-AFRICAN CONGRESS IN 1974. THE WIDELY RESPECTED STATESMAN IS AN ARDENT ADVOCATE OF PAN-AFRICAN BROTHERHOOD. HE IS A CULTURAL HERO IN TANZANIA

1979 GEO L. LEE FEATURE SERVICE

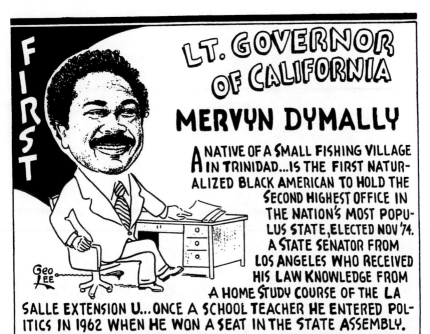

LT. GOVERNOR OF CALIFORNIA

MERVYN DYMALLY

A NATIVE OF A SMALL FISHING VILLAGE IN TRINIDAD...IS THE FIRST NATURALIZED BLACK AMERICAN TO HOLD THE SECOND HIGHEST OFFICE IN THE NATION'S MOST POPULUS STATE, ELECTED NOV '74. A STATE SENATOR FROM LOS ANGELES WHO RECEIVED HIS LAW KNOWLEDGE FROM A HOME STUDY COURSE OF THE LA SALLE EXTENSION U...ONCE A SCHOOL TEACHER HE ENTERED POLITICS IN 1962 WHEN HE WON A SEAT IN THE STATE ASSEMBLY.

Geo Lee

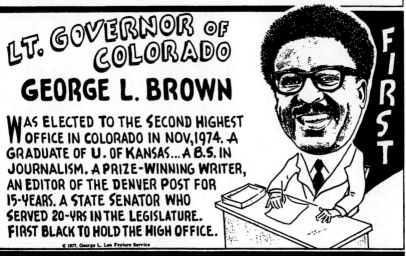

LT. GOVERNOR OF COLORADO

GEORGE L. BROWN

W AS ELECTED TO THE SECOND HIGHEST OFFICE IN COLORADO IN NOV, 1974. A GRADUATE OF U. OF KANSAS...A B.S. IN JOURNALISM. A PRIZE-WINNING WRITER, AN EDITOR OF THE DENVER POST FOR 15-YEARS. A STATE SENATOR WHO SERVED 20-YRS IN THE LEGISLATURE. FIRST BLACK TO HOLD THE HIGH OFFICE.

BISHOP HAROLD R. PERRY
OF NEW ORLEANS, LA.

FIRST BLACK IN THE U.S. TO BE CONSECRATED A BISHOP IN THE ROMAN CATHOLIC CHURCH SINCE 1875. BORN IN LAKE CHARLES, LA., HE ENTERED ST. AUGUSTINE'S SEMINARY AT THE AGE OF 14. LATER STUDIED AT BAY ST. LOUIS, MISS., TECHNY, ILL., AND EAST TROY, WIS. ON JAN 6, 1944 HE WAS ORDAINED AS A PRIEST.

Geo. Lee

IN 1952 HE BUILT A CHURCH RECTORY AND SCHOOL IN BROUSSARD, LA. IN 1958 HE WAS NAMED RECTOR OF THE DIVINE WORD SEMINARY IN BAY ST. LOUIS. IN 1963 HE BECAME THE FIRST BLACK TO DELIVER THE INVOCATION AT THE OPENING SESSION OF A U.S. CONGRESS. HE WAS THE FIRST TO BE NAMED PROVINCIAL SUPERIOR OF THE SOUTHERN PROVINCE OF THE DIVINE WORD SEMINARIES (11 STATES) IN 1964. WHILE IN ROME IN 1965 HE WAS INVITED TO THE VATICAN AND ASKED IF HE WOULD ACCEPT THE ELEVATION TO BISHOP — HE ACCEPTED!

A SHINING JEWEL

JEWEL LaFONTANT

MRS. LaFONTANT WAS BORN IN CHICAGO, AND EDUCATED IN THE PUBLIC SCHOOLS. SHE WENT TO OBERLIN COLLEGE IN OHIO, WHERE SHE RECEIVED-B.A.DEGREE-IN POLITICAL SCIENCE. THEN TO THE UNIVER- SITY OF CHICAGO FOR HER DOCTOR OF LAW DEGREE. HER LEGAL CAREER BEGAN AS A TRIAL ATTORNEY FOR THE LEGAL AID BUREAU OF UNITED CHARITIES OF CHICAGO. LATER BECAME THE FIRST BLACK WOMAN APPOINTED AN ASSISTANT U.S. DISTRICT ATTORNEY... AND THE FIRST ADMITTED TO THE CHICAGO BAR ASSOCIATION. MRS. LaFONTANT HAS ALWAYS BEEN ACTIVE IN REPUBLICAN POLITICS AND WAS ONCE CIVIL RIGHTS ADVISOR TO AMBASSADOR HENRY CABOT LODGE. FOLLOW- ING IN THE FOOTSTEPS OF HER LATE FATHER, C. FRANCIS STRADFORD, SHE IS A SENIOR PARTNER IN THE LAW FIRM HE ONCE

Geo LEE

RECEIVED AN HONORARY LAW DEGREE FROM CEDAR CREST COLLEGE IN PENNSYLVANIA (1973)

I DIG I DIG

SUPREME COURT

EDUCATION BABY!

U.S. DEPUTY SOLICITOR GENERAL!

HEADED. IN 1969 WAS APPOINTED TO THE U.S. ADVISORY COMMISSION ON INTERNATIONAL AND CULTURAL AF- FAIRS AND BECAME ITS VICE-PRESIDENT. IN 1972, NAMED U.S. REPRESENTATIVE TO THE UNITED NATIONS. ON MAR 19, 1973 BECAME THE FIRST WOMAN TO REPRESENT THE FEDERAL GOVERN- MENT BEFORE THE SUPREME COURT AS A... U.S. DEPUTY SOLICITOR GENERAL. A BRILLIANT LAWYER HER HONORS AND AWARDS ARE NUMEROUS. MRS. LaFONTANT IS ON THE BOARD OF DIRECTORS OF... JEWEL CO, TWA AND FOOTE, CONE & BELDING. BEAUTIFUL!

© 1974 George L. Lee Feature Service

WHAT A DIFFERENCE A DAY MAKES

DINAH WASHINGTON
1924 - 1964

KNOWN TO THE MUSIC WORLD OF BLUES AS "THE QUEEN." BORN IN TUSCALOOSA, ALA., AS RUTH LEE JONES. RAISED IN THE GHETTOS OF CHICAGO. HER CAREER BEGAN WITH LIONEL HAMPTON'S BAND AFTER SHE WON AN AMATEUR CONTEST AT THE REGAL THEATRE AND CHANGED HER NAME TO DINAH WASHINGTON. SHE SANG HER WAY TO STARDOM AND WAS COMPARED WITH BESSIE SMITH-THE GREATEST BLUES SINGER. DINAH RECORDED OVER 300 SONGS A TREMENDOUS BOX-OFFICE ATTRACTION EARNING AS HIGH AS $150,000. (A YR) BIG HITS - WHAT A DIFFERENCE A DAY MAKES; EVIL GAL BLUES; SALTY PAPA BLUES AND BLOW TOP BLUES.

Geo LEE

CHALKY WRIGHT

EX-FEATHER-WEIGHT CHAMP

WHO WON THE FEATHERWEIGHT TITLE FROM JOEY ARCHIBALD ON SEPT 11, 1941 IN MADISON SQ., GARDEN, NYC. AT THE TIME HE WAS KNOWN AS THE "OLD MAN" WITH 16-YEARS OF BOXING. BORN IN DURANGO, MEXICO IN 1912. AT 9 HIS FAMILY MOVED TO COLTON, CALIF., AND IN DESPERATION FROM POVERTY HE TURNED TO THE RING. A NATURAL 126-POUNDER HE WAS SO GOOD THAT HE HAD TO FIGHT LIGHTWEIGHTS (135lbs); WELTER-WEIGHTS (147lbs), BEFORE A CHANCE AT THE **TITLE...**

© 1975 George L. Lee Feature Service

FROM TEACHER TO NATION LEADER

Geo Lee

ROBERT G. MUGABE

PRIME MINISTER OF THE NEW AFRICAN NATION-ZIMBABWE, ONCE KNOWN AS RHODESIA. ELECTED APRIL 18, 1980 TO HEAD ITS NEW DESTINY. BORN INTO THE SHONA TRIBE IN 1924 THE SON OF A CARPENTER. RAISED A STRICT CATHOLIC AND SELF-EDUCATED. HE EARNED A DEGREE FROM FT. HARE UNIV., IN SOUTH AFRICA WHERE HE FIRST WAS EXPOSED TO BLACK NATIONALISM. HE BECAME A TEACHER AND TAUGHT IN RHODESIA, GHANA AND ZAMBIA. ALTHOUGH MUGABE EARNED MORE DEGREES HE SOON REALIZED THE DIFFERENCES OF HIS PAY AND WHITE TEACHERS. IN 1960, JOINED JOSHUA NKOMO AND HIS NATIONALISTS. IN 1963 LEFT NKOMO TO FORM THE ZANU (ZIMBABWE AFRICAN NAT'L UNION) WITH REV. N. SITHOLE. HE SPENT 9-YEARS IN JAIL, WENT TO MOZAMBIQUE AND FORMED HIS OWN ZANU. MUGABE'S GUERRILLA'S WERE A BIG FACTOR IN ZIMBABWE'S INDEPENDENCE!

FEAR NOT! DO NOT FLEE!

MUGABE URGED THE WHITES TO STAY AND LIVE WITH THE BLACKS IN A NEW SOCIETY!

1980 GEO L. LEE FEATURE SERVICE

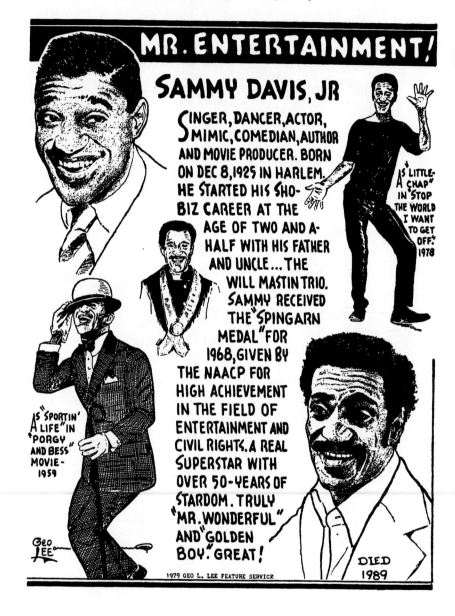

MR. ENTERTAINMENT!

SAMMY DAVIS, JR

SINGER, DANCER, ACTOR, MIMIC, COMEDIAN, AUTHOR AND MOVIE PRODUCER. BORN ON DEC 8, 1925 IN HARLEM. HE STARTED HIS SHO-BIZ CAREER AT THE AGE OF TWO AND A-HALF WITH HIS FATHER AND UNCLE... THE WILL MASTIN TRIO. SAMMY RECEIVED THE "SPINGARN MEDAL" FOR 1968, GIVEN BY THE NAACP FOR HIGH ACHIEVEMENT IN THE FIELD OF ENTERTAINMENT AND CIVIL RIGHTS. A REAL SUPERSTAR WITH OVER 50-YEARS OF STARDOM. TRULY "MR. WONDERFUL" AND "GOLDEN BOY." GREAT!

AS "LITTLE-CHAP" IN "STOP THE WORLD I WANT TO GET OFF." 1978

AS "SPORTIN' LIFE" IN "PORGY AND BESS" MOVIE- 1959

GEO LEE

DIED 1989

1979 GEO L. LEE FEATURE SERVICE

FAMED PIANIST

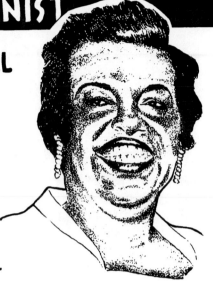

WINIFRED ATWELL

WHO WAS HAILED AS THE MOST POPULAR PIANIST IN ENGLAND IN 1955 WAS ONCE A DRUGGIST IN HER FATHER'S DRUG STORE. BORN IN TRINIDAD, SHE STARTED PLAYING THE PIANO AT 5, GAVE A CHOPIN RECITAL AT 6. IN 1945 SHE WENT TO N.Y.C. TO STUDY...THEN TO LONDON TO STUDY BACH UNDER A FAMOUS TEACHER. TO PAY FOR HER STUDIES SHE TURNED TO PLAYING JAZZ IN CLUBS...SHE HIT

Geo Lee

THE BIGTIME IN 1951 WHEN SHE BOUGHT AN OLD "SALOON PIANO" FOR 30 SHILLINGS ($4.20) AND RECORDED "BLACK AND WHITE RAG" AS A GIMMICK...IT WAS A SMASH HIT AND SHE WENT ON TO BE A TOP STAR...PLAYING BOOGIE ON HER "SALOON PIANO" AND CLASSICAL RENDITIONS ON A GRAND PIANO. THE FIRST FEMALE PIANIST IN ENGLISH HISTORY TO HEADLINE A MAJOR VARIETY BILL.

© 1974 George L. Lee Feature Service

FOUGHT FOR DEMOCRACY

PFC. JACK THOMAS
OF ALBANY, GA.

A FIGHTING INFANTRYMAN, ONE OF 2600 BLACK GIs WHO VOLUNTEERED IN THE SPRING OF 1945 TO FIGHT ALONGSIDE THEIR WHITE COMRADES IN 7-INFANTRY DIVISIONS ON THE WESTERN FRONT. WAS AWARDED THE DISTINGUISHED SERVICE CROSS FOR...EXTRAORDINARY HEROISM IN CONNECTION WITH MILITARY OPERATIONS

Geo Lee

THE NATION'S SECOND HIGHEST HONOR!

AGAINST THE ENEMY DURING ACTION NEAR HARVEGRODE, GERMANY. THE GEORGIA DOUGHBOY WAS A FIGHTER IN CO. E OF THE FAMOUS 60th (GO DEVIL) INFANTRY REGIMENT WHICH FOUGHT WITH THE 9th INFANTRY DIVISION OF GENERAL HODGES' FAMED U.S. FIRST ARMY.

FIRST IN CANADA'S HOUSE OF COMMONS

Geo LEE

LINCOLN ALEXANDER

THE FIRST BLACK TO BE ELECTED TO CANADA'S PARLIAMENT IN OTTAWA. A NATIVE OF HAMILTON, ONTARIO. HE STUDIED LAW IN TORONTO AND SERVED IN THE CANADIAN AIRFORCE DURING WORLD WAR II. LATER BECAME INTERESTED IN POLITICS. HE LOST IN HIS FIRST ATTEMPT IN 1965 BUT WON IN 1968, ON THE PRO- GRESSIVE CONSERVATIVE TICKET.

HON. LYNDEN O. PINDLING

FIRST BLACK PRIME MINISTER OF THE BAHAMAS, 700 ISLANDS OFF THE COAST OF FLORIDA. HE HEADS THE FIRST ALL-BLACK GOVERNMENT IN ITS OVER 300-YEAR HISTORY (1967). BORN IN NASSAU (1930) HE RE- CEIVED HIS HIGHER EDUCATION AT THE UNIVERSITY OF LONDON AND HIS LAW FROM MIDDLE TEMPLE. HE WAS ADMITTED TO THE ENGLISH BAR IN 1953. HE ONCE DANCED PROFESSIONALLY.

THE BAHAMAS

PARADISE

© 1947 George L. Lee Feature Service

SEE HOW THEY RUN

MARY ELIZABETH VROMAN

ONE OF AMERICA'S HIGHLY TALENTED WOMEN WRITERS. BORN IN BUFFALO, N.Y., SHE GREW UP IN ANTIGUA, W.I. RETURNING TO THE U.S., SHE ATTENDED ALABAMA STATE TEACHERS COLLEGE IN MONTGOMERY. WHILE TEACHING IN RURAL ALABAMA SHE WROTE HER FIRST SHORT STORY-"SEE HOW THEY RUN", A STORY ABOUT THE CHILDREN. IN 1952 IT WAS PUBLISHED IN THE LADIES' HOME JOURNAL. SHE GAINED NATIONAL RECOGNITION AND WON THE CELEBRATED "CHRISTOPHER AWARD." MGM STUDIOS BOUGHT THE SCREEN RIGHTS AND PRODUCED THE MOVIE "BRIGHT ROAD," STARRING DOROTHY DANDRIDGE AND HARRY BELAFONTE. MISS VROMAN SERVED AS THE ... TECHNICAL ADVISER AND HELPED TO WRITE THE SCREENPLAY. THE FIRST BLACK WOMAN MEMBER OF THE SCREEN WRITERS GUILD. HER CAREER WAS CUT SHORT BY DEATH IN BROOKLYN AT 42 (1967).

Geo Lee

1970 GEO L. LEE FEATURE SERVICE

3 - BOOKS ~
ESTHER
SHAPED TO ITS PURPOSE
HARLEM SUMMER

A GIFTED TEACHER WHO GAVE HER ALL. SHE ALSO TAUGHT IN CHICAGO AND NEW YORK ... ALSO WROTE MANY ARTICLES AND SHORT STORIES.

IN PRIVATE LIFE, WIFE OF DR. OLIVER M. HARPER, BROOKLYN DENTIST.

°1952 CHRISTOPHER AWARD °
PRESENTED TO
ELIZABETH VROMAN
FOR HER MAGAZINE STORY
SEE HOW THEY RUN
AND FOR THE INSPIRATION AND HOPE
IT PROVIDED A VAST AUDIENCE.
THIS OUTSTANDING WORK IS LIVING
PROOF OF THE POWER OF CREATIVE
ARTS UNDER GOD TO CHANGE THE
WORLD FOR THE BETTER.

♪ C'EST SI BON ♪♪

EARTHA KITT

WHO ROSE FROM A HUMBLE BE-GINNING IN NORTH, S.C. TO FAME AND FORTUNE AS A SINGER, DANCER AND ACTRESS. HER CAREER STARTED WITH THE KATHERINE DUNHAM'S DANCERS IN THE U.S. AND EUROPE. IN PARIS SHE SANG IN BISTROS AND PLAYED HELEN OF TROY IN "FAUST" OPPOSITE ORSON WELLES. BECAME A HIT IN THE BROADWAY REVUE "NEW FACES" IN 1952. AT THE AGE OF 26 SHE PLAYED A 15-YEAR OLD GIRL IN THE BROADWAY PLAY... "MRS. PATTERSON." SHE RECEIVED THE STAR AND CROSS AWARD OF THE AMERICAN INT'L ACADEMY-THE FIRST ENTERTAINER. PLAYED A CAT ROLE IN 1957 IN "SHINBONE ALLEY." EARTHA CAN SING IN FRENCH, TURKISH, GERMAN, ITALIAN AND SPANISH.... ONE OF HER HITS... C'EST SI BON."

THE TREMENDOUS STAR STARTED THE KITTSVILLE YOUTH FOUNDATION IN 1966 IN WATTS (L.A.CALIF), A SCHOOL OF DANCE FOR THE UNDERPRIVILEGED AND FINANCED BY...EARTHA KITT. A WARM HEARTED HUMANITARIAN....

Geo LEE

1973 George L. Lee Feature Service

115

FROM ENLISTED SOLDIER TO GENERAL

VIETNAM HEROISM: 2 SILVER STARS FOR VALOR, 2 PURPLE HEARTS-WITH THE 101st AIRBORNE DIV.

LT. GEN. JULIUS W. BECTON JR

A BRILLIANT MILITARY CAREER THAT STARTED IN HIGH SCHOOL IN ARDMORE, PA. GRADUATING IN JUNE 1944 AND A PRIVATE IN THE ARMY AIR CORPS HE REPORTED TO KEESLER FIELD, MISS., FOR TRAINING. AN EYE DEFICIENCY ENDED HIS HOPES OF BECOMING A FIGHTER PILOT. THE ARMY REASSIGNED HIM TO McDILL AIR BASE, FL., AS AN AVIATION ENGINEER. THE DUTIES PROVED BORING. HE WAS MADE UNIT CLERK. BECTON APPLIED FOR OFFICER CANDIDATE

Geo LEE

SCHOOL AND BECAME A 2nd LIEUT., (1945) AT FT. BENNING, GA. IN 1946 HE SERVED AS A SIGNAL OFFICER IN THE PHILIPPINES. IN 1947, LEFT THE MILITARY TO ENTER MUHLENBERG COLLEGE. RETURNED TO THE ARMY AS A 1st LIEUT., (1948). HE SOUGHT MORE EDUCATION. A B.S. DEGREE FROM PRAIRIE VIEW A & M COLL., (1960). M.A. FROM U of MARYLAND. A GRADUATE OF ARMED FORCES STAFF COLLEGE AND THE NATIONAL WAR COLLEGE.

1983 Geo L. Lee Feature Service

IN 1982, BECTON, DEPUTY COMMANDING GENERAL FOR TRAINING, U.S. ARMY TRAINING AND DOCTRINE COMMAND RECEIVED THE KNIGHT COMMANDER'S CROSS OF THE ORDER OF MERIT, W. GERMANY'S HIGHEST MILITARY AWARD.

BECTON

IN OCT. 1978 HE BECAME COMMANDING GENERAL OF THE VIIth CORPS, THE LARGEST, MOST POWERFUL COMBAT CORPS, OVER 80,000 - FRANKFURT, W. GER.

PRESIDENT OF MICHIGAN STATE U.

CLIFTON R. WHARTON JR
NATIVE OF BOSTON, MASS.

FIRST BLACK TO BE PRESIDENT OF A MAJOR AMERICAN UNIVERSITY IN THE 20TH CENTURY. A BRILLIANT STUDENT, HIS EARLY EDUCATION WAS AT BOSTON LATIN SCHOOL. HE ENTERED HARVARD AT 16 AND WAS A FOUNDER AND FIRST SECRETARY OF THE U.S. NATIONAL STUDENTS ASSN. IN 1947 HE GRADUATED WITH A B.A. DEGREE IN HISTORY. HE EARNED HIS MASTERS FROM THE JOHN HOPKINS SCHOOL OF INTERNATIONAL STUDIES, THE FIRST

Geo Lee

BLACK. HE WAS ALSO THE FIRST BLACK TO RECEIVE A PH.D IN ECONOMICS FROM THE U OF CHICAGO. AN EXPERT IN THE FIELD OF ECONOMICS HE WAS VICE-PRES., OF THE AGRICULTURAL DEVELOPMENT COUNCIL THAT DEVELOPED PROGRAMS IN LATIN AMERICA AND SOUTHEAST ASIA. THE SON OF THE FIRST BLACK MINISTER TO RUMANIA AND AMBASSADOR TO NORWAY. DR. WHARTON ASSUMED HIS DUTIES AS HEAD OF THE 45,000 STUDENT-BODY OF **MSU** IN JANUARY, 1970.

© 1971 George L. Lee Feature Service

SINGER - ACTOR - FILM PRODUCER

HARRY BELAFONTE

THE INTERNATIONAL SINGING STAR WHO IS BEST KNOWN FOR HIS CALYPSO FOLK SONGS. A SENSITIVE ARTIST, OUTSPOKEN ACTIVIST, HUMANITARIAN AND A GOOD FILM PRODUCER. BORN IN HARLEM IN 1927, OF JAMAICAN PARENTS. DURING HIS EARLY LIFE HE SPENT 5-YEARS IN JAMAICA. RETURNED TO HARLEM AND SOON REALIZED THAT GANGS WERE NOT FOR HIM. HE JOINED THE NAVY IN 1944. STUDIED ACTING AT N.Y's DRAMATIC WORKSHOP. ATTENDED THE NEW SCHOOL FOR SOCIAL RESEARCH AND THE AMERICAN NEGRO THEATRE WITH SIDNEY POITIER. ONE DAY IN JAN 1949 HE DROPPED INTO THE ROYAL ROOST CAFE IN MANHATTAN TO LISTEN TO WOODY HERMAN'S BAND. DURING A BREAK THE PRODUCER ASKED HARRY TO SING... A SINGING CAREER BEGAN ...BUT IT DIDN'T LAST LONG. HE DID NOT LIKE TO SING POPULAR MUSIC. HE STUDIED FOLK MUSIC AND SOON A BIG SUCCESS. HIT RECORDINGS, NIGHT CLUB OFFERS AND MOVIE ROLES.

IN 1960 WON TV'S "EMMY" FOR OUTSTANDING VARIETY OR MUSICAL PERFORMANCE IN HIS "TONIGHT WITH BELAFONTE". THE FIRST BLACK TO WIN THE... COVETED GOLD TROPHY. IN 1957 HIS FILM COMPANY MADE THEIR FIRST FILM "END OF THE WORLD". LATER "ODDS AGAINST TOMORROW," "THE ANGEL LEVINE" AMONG HIS CREDITS.

1981 GEO L. LEE FEATURE SERVICE

MEDAL OF HONOR HERO

WHITE HOUSE CEREMONY
MAR, 1967

PRESIDENT LYNDON JOHNSON AWARDS SPC/6 LAWRENCE JOEL WITH THE HIGHEST U.S. MILITARY HONOR THE CONGRESSIONAL MEDAL OF HONOR FOR....

"CONSPICUOUS GALLANTRY AND INTREPIDITY IN ACTION AT THE RISK OF HIS LIFE ABOVE AND BEYOND THE CALL OF DUTY"
VIETNAM – NOV 8, 1965

SPC/6 LAWRENCE JOEL

A NATIVE OF WINSTON-SALEM, N.C., WHO DROPPED OUT OF HIGH SCHOOL TO JOIN THE ARMY IN 1946 AND SEE THE WORLD. DURING THE VIETNAM WAR HE SERVED AS A "MEDICAL AIDE", IN COMPANY "C", 1ST BATTALION (AIR-BORNE) 503 INFANTRY. ON NOV 8, 1965 COMPANY "C" WAS AMBUSHED BY THE VIET CONG. FOR MORE THAN 24-HOURS OF CONTINUOUS AID TO THE WOUNDED UNDER HEAVY MACHINE GUN FIRE EVEN AFTER HE HAD BEEN HIT IN THE LEG AND HIP. DESPITE HIS WOUNDS HE SAVED 13 MEN UNTIL HIS SUPPLIES GAVE OUT. HIS DARING COURAGE WAS AN INSPIRATION TO ALL. JOEL, THE FIRST MEDIC IN VIETNAM TO WIN THE MEDAL OF HONOR AND THE 46th BLACK IN U.S. MILITARY HISTORY!

GEO LEE

GENTLEMAN FROM PENNSYLVANIA

ROBERT N.C. NIX
OF PHILADELPHIA

WHO SERVED 10-TERMS IN THE U.S. CONGRESS AND THE 4th BLACK CONGRESSMAN SINCE 1875. HE WAS ELECTED TO THE 85th CONGRESS IN 1958 AND SERVED THE 2nd DISTRICT, (D., PA.) FOR 20-YEARS. A NATIVE OF ORANGEBURG, S.C. HE WAS ONCE DEPUTY STATE'S ATTORNEY-GENERAL (PA.). REP. NIX FOUGHT FOR CIVIL RIGHTS OF HIS CONSTITUENTS AND BECAME CHAIRPERSON OF THE POST OFFICE AND CIVIL SERVICE COMM. PRESIDENT CARTER

MR. SPEAKER! I ASK UNANIMOUS CONSENT THAT THE OATH OF OFFICE BE ADMINISTERED TO THE GENTLEMAN FROM PENNSYLVANIA–MR. ROBERT N.C. NIX!

GEO LEE

LAUDED NIX FOR HIS ACTIVE WORK ON KEY ISSUES IN 1978. A MEMBER OF THE INT'L RELATIONS COMM... THE INT'L DEVELOPMENT AND AFRICA SUBCOMMITTEES. DURING HIS TENURE ON CAPITOL HILL HE HAD ONE OF THE BEST ATTENDANCE RECORDS. ONCE A PHILADELPHIA TRIAL LAWYER.

ON JUNE 4, 1958 REP. FRANCIS E. WALTER OF PENNA., AROSE AND ADDRESSED THE HOUSE!

1979 GEO L. LEE FEATURE SERVICE

BROCK PETERS

FOLK-SINGER, BROADWAY AND MOTION PICTURE ACTOR WAS BORN GEORGE FISHER IN NEW YORK CITY IN 1929. HIS FATHER A SENGALESE AND MOTHER A WEST INDIAN. EDUCATED AT NEW YORK'S FAMED MUSIC AND ARTS HIGH SCHOOL. HE STUDIED PHYSICAL ED., AT C.C.N.Y. BUT QUIT WHEN HE WON A ROLE IN A ROAD PRODUCTION OF PORGY AND BESS IN 1949, HIS FIRST MAJOR BREAK. BROCK WAS ONCE A MEMBER OF THE FAMED DePAUR INFANTRY CHORUS. ALTHO HE HAD A DEGREE OF SUCCESS ON AND OFF-BROADWAY, RECORDINGS AND BRITISH FILMS, THE L-SHAPED ROOM "AND "HEA-

Geo LEE

VENS ABOVE"...IT WASN'T UNTIL HIS FIRST STRAIGHT DRAMATIC ROLE IN THE FILM "TO KILL A MOCKING BIRD" WITH GREGORY PECK THAT HE REALLY ATTRACTED ATTENTION. HE WON THE 1963 AWARD OF THE ALL-AMERICAN PRESS ASSN., FOR "BEST SUPPORTING ACTOR." IN 1969 HE PLAYED THE LEAD IN THE ROAD COMPANY OF "THE GREAT WHITE HOPE." IN 1974 HE CO-PRODUCED THE MOVIE... "FIVE ON THE BLACK HAND SIDE" A BLACK COMEDY.

ARTHUR GODFREY'S TALENT SCOUT PROGRAM

BROCK A BARITONE WON FIRST PRIZE ON ARTHUR GODFREY'S CBS TALENT SCOUTS IN 1953 SINGING "900 MILES." THIS LED TO A RECORDING CONTRACT WITH COLUMBIA.

MR. CONGRESSMAN FROM N.Y.

CHARLES B. RANGEL

THE MAN WHO DEFEATED THE "LEGEND", ADAM CLAYTON POWELL IN THE HARLEM DEMOCRATIC PRIMARY ELECTION, JUNE 1970 BY ONLY 150 VOTES. ELECTED TO CONGRESS FROM N.Y. 19th DIST.,(NOV, '70). BORN AND REARED IN HARLEM. DROPPED OUT OF HIGH SCHOOL TO JOIN THE ARMY. FOUGHT IN KOREA WINNING MANY AWARDS INCLUDING U.S. AND KOREAN PRESIDENTIAL CITATIONS (1948-52). RETURNED TO HARLEM. FINISHED HI-SCHOOL, ENTERED NYU ON THE G.I. BILL AND GRADUATED ON THE DEAN'S LIST. EARNED

A LAW DEGREE AT ST. JOHN'S U., (1960). PASSED THE N.Y. BAR THEN APPOINTED ASS'T U.S. ATTY.,('61). ELECTED TO N.Y. STATE ASSEMBLY (1966-70). MR. RANGEL HAS SERVED WITH DISTINCTION IN CONGRESS. A MEMBER OF THE HOUSE WAYS AND MEANS COMM, ('75). SERVED AS CHAIRMAN OF THE BLACK CAUCUS (1974-75). FIRST BLACK CHAIRMAN OF THE WAYS AND MEANS SUBCOMM. ON HEALTH ('77).

• SELECT COMMITTEE ON CRIME
• SELECT COMMITTEE ON NARCOTICS ABUSE AND CONTROL
• MEMBER JUDICIARY COMM., WHO VOTED ARTICLES OF IMPEACHMENT AGAINST PRES. NIXON
• MAJORITY REGIONAL WHIP FOR N.Y. STATE

1982 ©EO L. LEE FEATURE SERVICE

122

MULTI-TALENT

GEOFFREY HOLDER

DIRECTOR OF THE BROAD-
WAY MUSICAL "THE W·I·Z",
WAS BORN IN TRINIDAD.
HE STARTED HIS CAREER
AS A DANCER AT THE AGE
OF 7, IN PORT-OF-SPAIN.
ARRIVED IN N.Y.C. IN 1953.
THE NEXT YEAR HE WAS A
FEATURE DANCER IN "HOUSE
OF FLOWERS" ON BROADWAY.
DANCED WITH HIS WIFE CARMEN
DE LAVALLADE WITH THE 'MET'
OPERA BALLET. HAD A FEATURED
ROLE IN THE MOVIE "DR. DOOLITTLE."

HE DANCES!
HE SINGS!
HE WRITES!
GOO LEE
COMPOSES
DESIGNS
HE PAINTS!

HE ACTS,
HE LECTURES!

AS AN ARTIST HE WAS ONCE A
GUGGENHEIM FELLOW. THE
6 FOOT 6 GEOFFREY IS WELL-
KNOWN AS THE "UNCOLA MAN"
IN TV COMMERCIALS, AMONG
HIS MANY. ALTHO HE STAMM-
ERED AS A BOY HE BECAME A
SPEAKER ON THE COLLEGE
CAMPUS TOUR WITH HIS ONE
MAN SHOW. TALENT GALORE!

© 1976 George L. Lee Feature Service

FAMOUS OPERA SOPRANO

Geo
LEE

MATTIWILDA DOBBS

WORLD FAMOUS COLORATURA SOPRANO. THE FIRST BLACK OPERA SINGER TO SING A PRINCIPAL ROLE IN THE LA SCALA OPERA HOUSE IN MILAN, ITALY. BORN IN ATLANTA, GA., A DAUGHTER OF THE DISTINGUISHED DOBBS FAMILY. STARTED CAREER AT 7 IN THE FIRST CONGREGATIONAL CHURCH CHOIR. A VOICE AND SPANISH GRADUATE OF SPELMAN COLLEGE AND COLUMBIA U. WON A MARIAN ANDERSON SINGING SCHOLARSHIP THEN A JOHN HAY WHITNEY FELLOWSHIP AND STUDIED IN PARIS AND SPAIN. IN 1951 WON THE INTERNATIONAL MUSIC COMPETITION AT GENEVA'S CONSERVATORY OF MUSIC. DEBUT AT "MET" IN 1956. SANG IN WORLD'S GREAT OPERA HOUSES. MARRIED IN 1957 TO SWEDISH BENGT JANZON AND LIVED IN SWEDEN FOR MANY YEARS. IN 1976 WAS NAMED A PROFESSOR OF MUSIC AT THE U. OF GEORGIA.

APPEARED AS "ELVIRA" IN "AN ITALIAN LADY IN ALGIERS" IN THE FAMED LA SCALA OPERA HOUSE (1953)

1980 GEO L. LEE FEATURE SERVICE

PHILIPPA SCHUYLER
OF NEW YORK CITY (1931-1967)

CHILD PRODIGY

Geo Lee

LEARNED HER ALPHABET AT 19 MONTHS. STARTED PIANO LESSONS AT 3. SHE AMAZED THE NATION WHEN AT AGE 4, PLAYED 10-SELECTIONS FROM MEMORY, 6 OF THEM HER OWN COMPOSITIONS IN THE 3rd ANNUAL NAT'L PIANO TOURN. (NYC. JUNE,1936)...BY 11 PHILIPPA HAD TO BE BARRED FROM THE N.Y. PHILHARMONIC SYMPHONY SOCIETY'S CONTEST...REASON..."TOO GOOD". AT 12, COMPOSED THE "MANHATTAN NOCTURNE" A SYMPHONY...AND SCORED IT FOR 100 INSTRUMENTS ...IT WAS PLAYED IN CARNEGIE HALL-1945. A BRILLIANT STUDENT SHE HAD AN IQ OF 185. PHILIPPA BECAME A JOURNALIST AND TRAVELLED EXTENSIVELY IN AFRICA. SHE WROTE SEVERAL BOOKS, INCLUDING "ADVENTURES IN BLACK AND WHITE". IN 1967 AS A CORRESPONDENT FOR THE MANCHESTER (N.H.) UNION LEADER IN VIETNAM SHE WAS KILLED IN AN ARMY HELICOPTER ACCIDENT IN DA NANG BAY.

FASTING FOR HUMANITY

DICK GREGORY

COMEDIAN TURNED ACTIVIST BACK FROM IRAN (1980) AND A FASTING, PRAYER-VIGIL FOR FREEDOM OF THE AMERICAN HOSTAGES, WEIGHING 97-POUNDS...ONCE WEIGHED 208 (1965). IN HIS NON-VIOLENT WAY, FIGHTS FOR HUMANITY! WORLD HUNGER, CIVIL RIGHTS, INDIAN FISHING-RIGHTS, VIETNAM. BORN IN ST. LOUIS IN 1932 AND RAISED ON RELIEF. A TRACK STAR IN HIGH SCHOOL, HE BROKE RECORDS AT SOUTHERN ILLINOIS U. SHOWED SKILL AS A COMIC IN ARMY TALENT CONTESTS. WORKED IN THE CHICAGO POST OFFICE.

Geo Lee

BEGAN COMIC CAREER AT THE CLUB ESQUIRE (CHGO) AT $10. A-NIGHT. HAD MANY UPS AND DOWNS. FINALLY... A BREAK..."THE PLAYBOY CLUB." AT 28, THE FIRST BLACK COMEDIAN TO MAKE THE BIG-TIME NIGHTCLUBS. DICK CHANGED FROM HUMOROUS TO HUMANISM. HE RUNS AND FASTS FOR JUST CAUSES.'

The COMIC

The SATIRIST

GREGORY RAN FOR PRESIDENT IN 1968. RECEIVED AN HONORARY DOCTORAL DEGREE FROM MACOLM X COLLEGE (CHGO) 1970. LECTURES AT COLLEGES. AUTHOR OF 10-BOOKS.

1980 GEO L. LEE FEATURE SERVICE

GODFATHER OF SOUL

JAMES BROWN

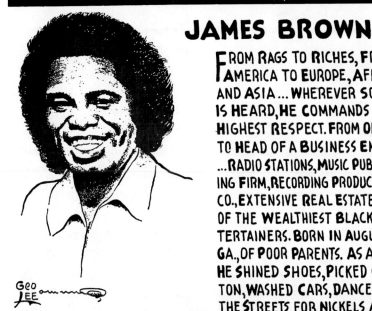

Geo
LEE

FROM RAGS TO RICHES, FROM AMERICA TO EUROPE, AFRICA AND ASIA...WHEREVER SOUL IS HEARD, HE COMMANDS THE HIGHEST RESPECT. FROM ORPHAN TO HEAD OF A BUSINESS EMPIRE. ...RADIO STATIONS, MUSIC PUBLISHING FIRM, RECORDING PRODUCTION CO., EXTENSIVE REAL ESTATE. ONE OF THE WEALTHIEST BLACK ENTERTAINERS. BORN IN AUGUSTA, GA., OF POOR PARENTS. AS A BOY HE SHINED SHOES, PICKED COTTON, WASHED CARS, DANCED ON THE STREETS FOR NICKELS AND DIMES. A 7th GRADE SCHOOL DROPOUT. AT 16 IN A REFORM SCHOOL, PAROLED AT 19. HE BEGAN TO SING SPIRITUALS IN A CHURCH. A FORMER BOXER TAUGHT BY EX-LIGHTWEIGHT CHAMP, BEAU JACK. BUT TURNED TO HIS VOCAL TALENTS. IN 1956 MADE HIS FIRST RECORDING,"PLEASE, PLEASE, PLEASE"...A MILLION-SELLER. A PHENOMENAL CAREER STARTED!

SOUL BROTHER No 1

A FEW OF HIS BIG HITS

"OUT OF SIGHT"
"DON'T BE A DROPOUT"
"REGRETS"
"POPCORN"
"COLD SWEAT"
"HOT"
"IT'S A MAN'S WORLD"
"GET ON THE GOOD FOOT"
"I MADE A MISTAKE" "WORLD WORLD"
"I'M BLACK AND I'M PROUD"

JAMES BROWN'S OVER 50 GOLD HITS! A SURE BET FOR MUSIC'S HALL OF FAME.

1981 GEO L. LEE FEATURE SERVICE

WORLD'S GREAT BASS·BARITONE

SIMON ESTES

WORLD RENOWNED SINGER, FIRST RECEIVED ACCLAIM WHEN HE WON THE MUNICH IN-TERNATIONAL COMPETITION IN 1965 AND WON MOSCOW'S INTERNATIONAL TCHAIKOVSKY VOCAL COMPETITION PRIZE (1966). A DECADE LATER WAS ACCEPTED BY AMERICA. BORN IN CENTER-VILLE, IOWA . HIS GRANDFATHER A SLAVE ESCAPED TO IOWA. HE STARTED SINGING IN THE CHUR-CH CHOIR. IN HIGH SCHOOL HE WON LETTERS IN SPORTS. STUDIED MEDICINE AND THEOLOGY AT THE U OF IOWA. THE VOICE INSTRUCTOR INSPIR-ED SIMON TO STUDY AND HE WON A SCHOLARSHIP TO JUILLIARD SCHOOL OF MUSIC. HE WENT TO EUROPE AND SOON BECAME A SOLOIST AND SANG IN THE OPERA CAPITOLS. HE HAS "PRESENCE." AMERICA RECOGNIZED HIS DISTINGUISHED TALENTS AND SOUGHT HIM FOR OPERA STAGES EVERYWHERE. TRULY A GREAT "VOICE" OF HIS TIME! BRAVO!

HE SINGS IN FRENCH, ITALIAN, GERMAN AND RUSSIAN AND ALSO SPEAKS!

SIMON MADE HIS "MET" OPERA DEBUT AS LANDGRAVE HERMANN IN "TANNHAUSER" ON JAN 4, 1982. IT WAS A SIGNIFICANT TRIUMPH!

DIPLOMAT·SCHOLAR·PROFESSOR

DONALD McHENRY

FORMER U.S. AMBASSADOR TO THE U.N. UNDER PRES. CARTER AND SUCCESSOR TO ANDREW YOUNG (1979). HE BECAME RESEARCH PROFESSOR OF DIPLOMACY AND INTERNATIONAL AFFAIRS AT GEORGE-TOWN UNIV., SCHOOL OF FOREIGN-SERV-ICE. BORN IN ST. LOUIS, MO., IN 1936 AND RAISED IN EAST ST. LOUIS, ILL. HIS FAMILY WAS POOR BUT HIS IDEALS WERE HIGH. IN HI-SCHOOL AN ACT-IVE HONOR STUDENT. A GRADUATE OF ILLINOIS STATE U., (1957) WITH A SOCIAL SCIENCE DEGREE; A MASTER'S IN SPEECH AND POLITICAL SCIENCE FROM SOUTHERN ILLINOIS U., (1959); TAUGHT ENGLISH AT HOWARD U., (1959-62). McHENRY JOINED THE STATE DEPT., IN 1963 AS A FOREIGN-SERVICE OFFICER. SERVED ON THIRD WORLD AFFAIRS AND THE INDEPENDENCE OF NAMBIA. ON LEAVE IN 1971 WAS A GUEST LECTURER AT GEORGETOWN U., A SCHOLAR AT BROOKINGS INSTI. IN 1973 JOINED THE CARNEGIE ENDOWMENT FOR INTERNAT-IONAL PEACE. A HUMAN RIGHTS ADVOCATE!

Geo LEE

McHENRY AT 42, THE 15th U.S. AMBASSADOR AND THE YOUNGEST TO THE U.N. AN EXPERT ON THE THIRD WORLD.

UNITED STATES

1982 GEO L. LEE FEATURE SERVICE

SOPRANO

MARGARET TYNES

WHO WAS A GUEST SOLOIST WITH THE OAKLAND SYMPHONY ORCHESTRA IN 1975 HAS PERFORMED THRU-OUT EUROPE AND THE U.S. SINCE HER FIRST MAJOR OPERATIC SUCCESS IN THE TITLE ROLE IN STRAUSS' "SALOME" AT THE SPOLETI FESTIVAL IN ITALY IN JULY 1961. THE OPERA "SALOME" MADE ITS FIRST APPEARANCE IN 1905

Geo
LEE

HER RICH, VOICE ZOOMING WITH EASE THRU THE PRECARIOUS LINES TO THE DELIGHT OF THOUSANDS... AN UNBELIEVABLE SALOME

AND WAS SO SHOCKING THAT IT WAS BANNED IN BERLIN, VIENNA, LONDON AND NEW YORK. THE FINAL SCENE SHOWS SALOME KISSING THE LIPS OF THE SEVERED HEAD OF JOHN THE BAPTIST. A FINE SINGER SHE IS A NATIVE OF VIRGINIA. THE DAUGHTER OF A CLERGYMAN, SHE HOLDS A MASTER'S DEGREE FROM COLUMBIA AND STUDIED AT JUILLIARD SCHOOL OF MUSIC (NY) AND MILAN, ITALY.

REGGAE SUPERSTAR

1945
1981

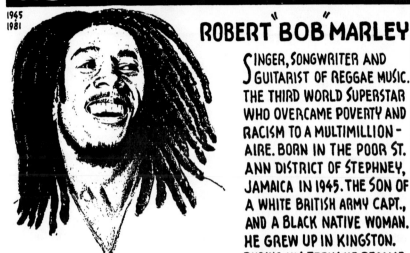

ROBERT "BOB" MARLEY

SINGER, SONGWRITER AND GUITARIST OF REGGAE MUSIC. THE THIRD WORLD SUPERSTAR WHO OVERCAME POVERTY AND RACISM TO A MULTIMILLION - AIRE. BORN IN THE POOR ST. ANN DISTRICT OF STEPHNEY, JAMAICA IN 1945. THE SON OF A WHITE BRITISH ARMY CAPT., AND A BLACK NATIVE WOMAN. HE GREW UP IN KINGSTON. DURING HIS TEENS HE BECAME FAMILIAR WITH THE RASTAFAR-IANISM RELIGIOUS MOVEMENT

THAT LATER INFLUENCED HIS MUSIC. HIS LYRICS CARRIED MESSAGES OF HIS TEACH-INGS. HIS REGGAE MUSIC...WEST INDIAN AND LATIN RHYTHMS IN A PATTERN OF 1-3 TIME AS OPPOSED TO 2-4 AMERICAN TIME. BOB STARTED HIS STAGE CAREER IN 1964 WHEN HE FORMED A GROUP, "THE WAILERS." CANCER CUT SHORT HIS BRILLIANT CAREER AT 36. A CHAMPION FOR EQUAL RIGHTS AND BLACK DIGNITY!

1983 Geo L. Lee Feature Service

HE SOLD MORE THAN 20 MILLION ALBUMS

WITH EARNINGS OVER 190 MILLION DURING HIS 17 YEAR CAREER.

ANDRE WATTS

CONCERT PIANIST

SON OF A BLACK G-I SOLDIER AND A HUNGARIAN MOTHER WAS BORN IN GERMANY AND LIVED IN U.S. ARMY POSTS. HIS FAMILY MOVED TO PHILADELPHIA WHEN HE WAS 8. ANDRE STARTED PIANO LESSONS AT 6, AND SOON HIS FUTURE WAS BRIGHT. AT 9 HE WON OVER 40 YOUNG PIANISTS TO PLAY A HAYDEN CONCERTO WITH THE PHILA., ORCHESTRA. HE WAS A SENSATION. HE STUDIED AT THE MUSICAL ACADEMY IN PHILA. BY 16 ANDRE WAS BRILLIANT AND HAD APPEARED WITH LEONARD BERNSTEIN FAMED CONDUCTOR OF THE N.Y. PHILHARMONIC (1963). HE GAINED WORLD RECOGNITION WHEN HE WAS ASKED TO SIT IN FOR

BRAVO! BRAVO!

VIRTUOSO GLENN GOULD AS SOLO-IST WITH THE N.Y. PHILHARMONIC. MR. GOULD HAD BECOME ILL. THE AUDIENCE WAS STUNNED WHEN THE TEEN-AGE BOY PLAYED LISZT'S E-FLAT CONCERTO FLAWLESSLY. A GENIUS OF THE PIANO. TODAY IN 1975, AT 29 HE IS A WORLD RENOWNED...CONCERT PIANIST!

Index

Index